Decoding Customer Value at the Bottom of the Pyramid

Decoding Customer Value at the Bottom of the Pyramid

An Urban India Marketing Perspective

Ritu Srivastava

BEP BUSINESS EXPERT PRESS

Decoding Customer Value at the Bottom of the Pyramid: An Urban India Marketing Perspective

First published in 2020 by
Business Expert Press, LLC
222 East 46th Street, New York, NY 10017
www.businessexpertpress.com

ISBN-13: 978-1-94897-611-4 (paperback)
ISBN-13: 978-1-94897-612-1 (e-book)

Business Expert Press Marketing Collection

Collection ISSN: 2150-9654 (print)
Collection ISSN: 2150-9662 (electronic)

Cover and interior design by Exeter Premedia Services Private Ltd., Chennai, India

First edition: 2020

10 9 8 7 6 5 4 3 2 1

Printed in the United States of America.

Abstract

Mature businesses across all advanced countries are struggling to find new markets as these countries are aging with the consequence that their domestic markets are either stagnant or growing very slowly. Their future seems to be destined to come from emerging markets, India being one of them. The challenge is especially high for business organizations that are leaders in their industry. Also, Marketing as a discipline has to serve the call of meeting societal and customer needs. The Indian market has been estimated huge in size, approximately $1.2 trillion in purchasing power parity for the households earning an annual income of less than $4,000. This comes to almost 830 million of Indian population of which 22 percent is urban India and 78 percent rural India, commonly referred to as Bottom of the Pyramid/Low Income/Subsistence Markets. While these markets offer immense business opportunities they also pose challenges because of their unique characteristics such as low incomes, geographical dispersion, heterogeneity in culture, poor transport, communication and media infrastructure, lack of education, different life styles compared to other income segments, lack of affordability and availability which are actually the effects of poverty. The needs of this segment have to be addressed by the corporate world but it might need a new approach with new business frameworks for implementation. The first most important thing that companies must understand is what constitutes value for this segment, how is it different from other segments and how can firms offer value through their market offerings, accordingly what could be the successful business models.

Decoding Customer Value at the Bottom of the Pyramid: An Urban India Perspective answers these questions through a practical, rigorous, and research-oriented way, written in a lucid and easy style for both practitioners and academicians for a quick grasp. This book would be a must read for Busineswws Executives across the globe with an interest in the low income customers in India. It will be a window for them to understand these customers and the perspective on value for them which can be incorporated in firm's products and services. This book is must for a Marketing Faculty in Indian Business Schools as this complements the existing Marketing core papers which fail to cover this side of the Indian

Reality for B School Participants. Together Business and Academia may start aligning to this customer segment which is seen as a challenge and both sides fail to organize themselves.

Keywords

value for bottom of the pyramid; low income; subsistence markets/india/ corporate

Contents

Preface ix

Acknowledgments xi

Chapter 1   Value—Multiple Perspectives 1

Chapter 2   Customer Perceived Value and Its Drivers in Urban
             BOP in India 39

Chapter 3   Delivering Customer Perceived Value at the Urban
             Bottom of the Pyramid in India 73

Chapter 4   Institutionalizing Customer Engagement at the Urban
             Bottom of the Pyramid in India: Research Insights 119

References 145

About the Author 159

Index 161

Preface

India is a country full of diversity. Home to more than one billion people, the diversity of cultures, incomes, and lifestyles can only be experienced by living in it. Being a management educationist and practitioner for over 17 years I realized that most of the academic discussion in B School Marketing classes happen around theories developed elsewhere largely developed economies catering to less than one percent of Indian population. As much as 75 percent of the population and context is not reflected in the Marketing Text which may lead to change or modification of existing theories.

While it was not possible to address all segments an effort has been made to start by addressing and understanding the needs of the segment which is next in line of market opportunity for corporate: The Urban India Bottom of the Pyramid segment. There is a firm belief that readers both from practice and academics side will find this book as their window to this segment. This may be seen as the start of the journey to a new business opportunity that would guide to the next more detailed steps to avail the opportunity and generate value both for the firm and the customers. Students, Company Executives, and Management Faculty can treat this as a handbook to refer for a broad overview of this customer and use the insights for their understanding.

This book has been written with a view to give readers, management practitioners, faculty and students, across the globe, a glimpse of the Urban Bottom of the Pyramid segment in an emerging market like India. The opportunity in this sector can only be converted into a win–win situation for all stakeholders. The need would be of understanding the customer and the segment closely by getting into it. The book revolves around the central theme of value. The first chapter covers multiple perspectives on value covering several frames: business, consumer, functional. It also talks on how value has evolved both in management discipline and subdiscipline of marketing. The chapter closes by bringing the reader from the organization side to the customer side. It then builds on the customer perceived value in the Urban Bottom of the Pyramid for India. The second chapter starts by listening to the Urban Bottom of the Pyramid Indian customers. Written as stories the chapter uses qualitative research technique of grounded theory to understand as to what constitutes customer perceived value in this segment and what are its main drivers. The third chapter constructs the framework to deliver customer perceived value in this segment and elaborates through business cases. The fourth chapter culminates by taking a long term approach to customer perceived value and converting it into lifelong customer engagement. It discusses the framework to institutionalize customer engagement at the Bottom of the Pyramid. The book serves as a reference on this segment in India. Comparisons to South Africa have been done wherever considered relevant. It has been written in a crisp and precise manner to serve as a source that can sensitize the readers to this segment. It may be seen as the first step of the journey.

I hope the readers have a pleasant and empathetic reading experience and look forward to the feedback.

Ritu Srivastava

01-05-2019

Acknowledgments

This book has been possible because of the millions of Indian people who are waiting to be heard by the marketing practitioners and academicians worldwide. They give inspiration to the thought that marketing is an inclusive science which carries the responsibility of catering to all the customers with respect. The difference needs to be acknowledged both in theory and practice.

I would like to express gratitude toward Lord Almighty and my guru who bestowed faith and energy to walk this path. A special thanks to my family who provided me encouragement and cooperation in the journey. Prof. Rajen Gupta, Prof. Neelu Bhullar, and Prof. Vibhava Srivastava, my colleagues at MDI Gurgaon have helped me with advice and discussion as and when required during the writing of the book. I thank them for the same.

CHAPTER 1

Value—Multiple Perspectives

Introduction

The concept of "Value" is not new to business and society. Over major civilizations and business revolutions the concept of value has undergone change. This chapter introduces different perspectives on value finally bringing to customer perceived value (CPV) by uniquely positioning it for Urban Bottom of the Pyramid context in an emerging market like India.

The Role of Business in Society

A society can be simply defined as a group of individual human beings making a living together. Over years to streamline live processes and channelize energy in a positive direction it takes a structure and is bound by certain rules to maintain discipline and decorum. History has seen several societies in the form of human civilizations. A society has a set of needs which comprises of individual and group needs. The individual needs can be best explained by the framework developed by Abraham Maslow 1943. Maslow's hierarchy of needs (Figure 1.1) is a motivational theory in psychology comprising a five-tier model of human needs, often depicted as hierarchical levels within a pyramid.

McLeod (2017) explains the theory where he mentions that needs lower down in the hierarchy must be satisfied before individuals can attend to needs higher up. From the bottom of the hierarchy upwards, the needs are: physiological, safety, love and belonging, esteem and self-actualization. This five-stage model can be divided into deficiency needs and

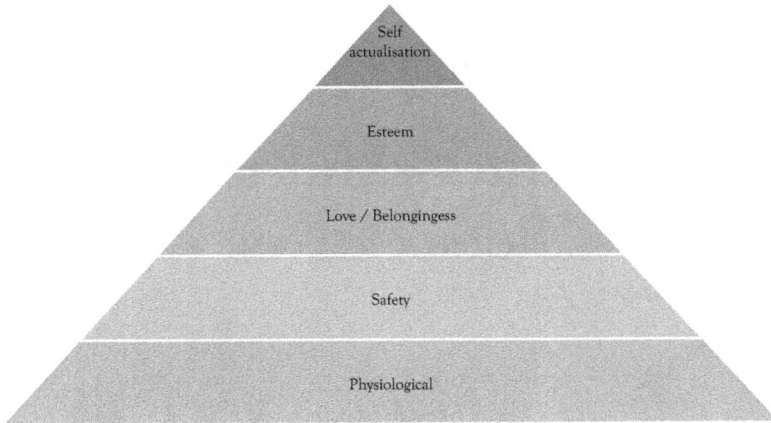

Figure 1.1 Maslow's hierarchy of needs

growth needs. The first four levels are often referred to as deficiency needs (D-needs), and the top level is known as growth or being needs (B-needs). Deficiency needs arise due to deprivation and are said to motivate people when they are unmet. Also, the motivation to fulfill such needs will become stronger the longer the duration they are denied. For example, the longer a person goes without food, the hungrier he will become. Maslow (1943) initially stated that individuals must satisfy lower level deficit needs before progressing on to meet higher level growth needs. However, he later clarified that satisfaction of a needs is not an "all-or-none" phenomenon, admitting that his earlier statements may have given "the false impression that a need must be satisfied 100 percent before the next need emerges" (1987, p. 69).

When a deficit need has been "more or less" satisfied it will go away, and our activities become habitually directed toward meeting the next set of needs that we have yet to satisfy. These then become our salient needs. However, growth needs continue to be felt and may even become stronger once they have been engaged. Growth needs do not stem from a lack of something, but rather from a desire to grow as a person. Once these growth needs have been reasonably satisfied, one may be able to reach the highest level called self-actualization. Every person is capable and has the desire to move up the hierarchy toward a level of self-actualization. Unfortunately, progress is often disrupted by a failure to meet lower level needs. Life experiences, including divorce and loss of a job, may cause an individual to fluctuate between levels of the hierarchy. Therefore, not everyone will move through the hierarchy in a uni-directional manner but may move back and forth between the different types of needs. Maslow (1943, 1954) stated that people are motivated to achieve certain needs and that some needs take precedence over others. Our most basic need is for physical survival, and this will be the first thing that motivates our behavior. Once that level is fulfilled the next level up is what motivates us, and so on. The original hierarchy of needs five-stage model includes;

1. Physiological needs—these are biological requirements for human survival, for example, air, food, drink, shelter, clothing, warmth, sex, and sleep.

   If these needs are not satisfied the human body cannot function optimally. Maslow considered physiological needs the most important as all the other needs become secondary until these needs are met.

2. Safety needs—protection from elements, security, order, law, stability, and freedom from fear.

3. Love and belongingness needs—after physiological and safety needs have been fulfilled; the third level of human needs is social and involves feelings of belongingness. The need for interpersonal relationships motivates behavior. Examples include friendship, intimacy, trust, and acceptance, receiving and giving affection and love. Affiliating, being part of a group (family, friends, and work).

4. Esteem needs—which Maslow classified into two categories:

   (a) esteem for oneself (dignity, achievement, mastery, and independence) and

   (b) the desire for reputation or respect from others (for example, status and prestige).

   Maslow indicated that the need for respect or reputation is most important for children and adolescents and precedes real self-esteem or dignity.

5. Self-actualization needs—realizing personal potential, self-fulfillment, seeking personal growth and peak experiences. A desire "to become everything one is capable of becoming" (Maslow 1987, p. 64).

Maslow continued to refine his theory based on the concept of a hierarchy of needs over several decades (Maslow 1943, 1962, 1987). Regarding the structure of his hierarchy, Maslow (1987) proposed that the order in the hierarchy "is not nearly as rigid" (p. 68) as he may have implied in his earlier description. Maslow noted that the order of needs might be flexible based on external circumstances or individual differences. For example, he noted that for some individuals, the need for self-esteem is more important than the need for love. For others, the need for creative fulfillment may supersede even the most basic needs. Maslow (1987) also pointed out that most behavior is multi-motivated and noted that "any behavior tends to be determined by several or all of the basic needs simultaneously rather than by only one of them" (p. 71).

As far as needs are concerned they are all the same at an individual level but there is difference in the ecosystem which is defined by the context. The group related needs comprise of feelings of belongingness, attachment which begin at an elementary level of a nuclear family moving into extended family, caste, geography, and so on. To meet the needs of societies and life, individuals take up roles and form organizations to implement those roles to meet the human needs. Thus the concept of enterprise is born. In its broadest sense an enterprise is an entity, organization, or undertaking that is created for commercial purposes or business ventures and requires human efforts for functioning. It is focused on providing goods and services keeping in view various aspects, such as financial, commercial, and industrial. An enterprise is composed of individuals and physical assets with a common goal of generating profits. As businesses evolve with time they compete and fight for their sustenance and survival along with time. Thus companies benefit society by nurturing relations with its multiple stakeholders, of which there may be many. Some stakeholders have a strong influence and are of fundamental importance to the survival of the company: these include employees, customers, and suppliers. The media, authorities, trade unions, and local residents are other stakeholders with a wide ranging influence. The stakeholders are thus classified as primary and secondary stakeholders. It is important for organizations to identify and understand their needs and relationship with each other so that the organization is able to sustain itself in the long run.

The basic objective of business is to develop, produce, and supply goods and services to customers. This has to be done in such a way as to allow companies to make a profit, which in turn demands far more than just skills in companies' own domains and processes. Astute entrepreneurs often demonstrate an almost intuitive understanding of the synergies that create success. The social skills of company owners, together with relationships maintained with customers, suppliers, and other business people, are always vital if companies are to be run well and developed with a view to the future. Companies improve their resources by developing materials and ideas. The goods and services produced must meet demands made by customers, other companies, or public institutions if companies are to survive. Profitability results when customers are prepared to pay more for goods and services than it costs to produce them. The ability to produce this kind of added value—profit—is the basic prerequisite for business, but it is also a foundation for prosperity in society. Only profitable companies are sustainable in the long term and capable of creating goods, services, processes, return on capital, work opportunities, and a tax base. This is what business does better than any other sector. Hence, companies' basic commercial operations are the primary benefit they bring to society. To summarize companies benefit society by:

- Supplying goods and services that customer cannot, or do not want to, produce themselves
- Creating jobs for customers, suppliers, distributors, and coworkers. These people make money to support themselves and their families, pay taxes, and use their wages to buy goods and services
- Continually developing new goods, services, and processes
- Investing in new technologies and in the skills of employees
- Building up and spreading international standards, for example, for environmental practices
- Spreading "good practice" in different areas, such as the environment and workplace safety

As one of the four factors of production, enterprise has the responsibility of bringing the other three together, that is, land, labor, and capital.

Manufacturing businesses typically start with the four factors of production. Services are construed slightly differently where people and processes take a prominent role. The role of the enterprise is to utilize the rest of the three factors, resources along with technology to create solutions for societal needs which is to be broken down as to be seen from two perspectives: firm and customers. It is important to consider here that these three factors of production are not bestowed equally over all the regions of mother earth but distributed unevenly. Thus the role of enterprise varies significantly in different contexts and their approach to value could be different at the micro level and macro level of economic development.

That society is a collection of individuals is true but this statement does not help in theoretical or practical purposes. It is important to define the relations between various actors in a particular social context. This would lead to understanding their economic development as well. Developing countries such as India remained colonies under the British rule for long. Their economies have a blend of both socialism and capitalism and that is why there are distinct different approaches and customer segments possible in the Indian population. It would not be proper to compare a capitalist approach to a socialist approach. Value in this book would follow more of a socialist approach rather than a capitalist approach popularly followed by Management schools and businesses in India that have developed largely on Western concepts.

Businesses Create Value

Businesses are the growth engine for a nation and that is how they generate value. Growth of the business may also be seen as an evidence of growth of individuals and nations. Businesses create economic growth which is related to development and progress of societies, economies, and nations, thus creating and enhancing value. The need is to build that infrastructure which provides value for each individual player within the larger value enhancing structure. The present system in India may be seen as comprising of business enterprises that utilize specialized skill and efforts of employees in return of salaries to deliver goods and services to the customer. The customers and the employees come from the same population. When competition enters the customer gets more choice, power and autonomy and in turn his demand for both quality and quantity goes up. This calls for even more skilled and specialized workforce which increases the salaries and disposable income. Investments also increase in business. But it is only the educated and qualified section of society that grows well in this system. In the process they do pull up the less educated segment that serves them well, but because of lack of education and professional skills their growth and integration with this system is at a slower pace. There is a big size of such a segment in India which may be classified under the bottom of the pyramid. Nthenge (2015) in his book elaborates that the bottom of the pyramid or BOP phrase has been coined by Prahlad and Hart (2002) that referred to four billion people living at almost $2 per day as per the World Economic Pyramid (WEP). India has been a home to a big number of this segment. The details of the bottom of the pyramid concept, characteristics, and evolution are provided in a later section of the chapter. It has become a necessity to work around the BOP markets and turn them from unorganized to organized. An individual or a group need has to be provided a solution by the organized business across market segments both from capitalist and socialist view. Socialist view talks of income equality across individuals, classes, and societies. Capitalist view talks of making more profits. Both are required as both the views talk of development and growth of an economy and would be important for this segment as well, but given a different market context, the differences would decide the marketing strategies directed toward inclusive growth, where Government also is an important actor.

The Strategic Concept of Value in a Firm

Maximizing shareholder value has been the ultimate goal of profit-making companies. Shareholders provide a company with the risk capital that enables managers to invest in the resources required to produce and sell goods and services or utilize in operations for the same. Risk capital is the capital that cannot be recovered if a company fails and goes bankrupt. Shareholders only provide risk capital when they believe that the company's management is committed to pursue strategies that promise a good return on their capital investment. Thus one of the goals of the company is to maximize shareholder value. Shareholder value means the returns that shareholders earn from purchasing the shares of the company. The returns originate from two sources;

1.   Capital appreciation in the value of a company's shares
2.   Dividend payments

Profitability of company is measured in several ways of which one is by the return that it makes on the capital invested in the enterprise. This is defined as the net profit over the capital invested in the firm. Capital invested includes both stockholder's equity plus debt owed to the creditors. Thus profitability is the result of how efficiently and effectively managers use the capital at their disposal to produce goods and services that satisfy customer needs. A company that uses its capital efficiently and effectively makes a positive return on invested capital. The profit growth of a company can be measured by the increase in net profit over time. This can be achieved by selling products in rapidly growing markets, gaining market share of the rivals, increasing the amount that it sells to the existing customers, expanding overseas, or diversifying profitably into new lines of businesses. Both of them combined, profitability and profit growth are main drivers of shareholder value. To boost this a company must pursue strategies that give it a competitive advantage over rivals. One of the key management challenges is to generate high profitability and increase the profits over time. Companies with either one of them alone would not be as highly valued by shareholders as companies achieving both. The management of companies also has to be alert to see that profitability does not go down with the increase in profits as even that is not perceived well by the shareholders. The function of Marketing along with other functions plays an important role to achieve this and addresses the concept of value and customers in its own way. It is therefore important to reflect on the Marketing thought as done in the following section.

Origin of Marketing Thought

Marketing is the art and science of choosing target markets and getting, keeping, and growing customers through creating, delivering, and communicating superior value.

—Kotler

Marketing as a science is the science of delivering value. The initial works in the early part of the 19th century focused on the changing economic conditions that encouraged writers to think about the marketing problems such as the price spread in farm products from producers to consumers and the increasing quantity of manufactured goods available in urban markets. The functional approach to marketing is what dominated the scene in 1970s and 1930s with major emphasis in decision making and profit orientation—concentrating around the marketing mix decisions with a focus on firm value. It then moved into the newer areas of marketing thought focusing on Quantitative Marketing, Marketing Systems, Marketing Channels, Logistics, and International Marketing, thus there was a more focused approach to theory development and conceptualization on Marketing Services side of it (Shaw and Tamilia 2001). It is relevant to touch upon the company's orientation to market place and the evolution of marketing thought with reference to value.

Company's Orientation to Market Place and Value

Marketing management has been defined as the conscious effort by a firm to achieve desired exchange of value with target markets. To achieve this there has to be a philosophy that should guide a company's marketing efforts, guide as to what relative weights should be given to the interests of the organization, the customers, and the society. Many a times these interest conflict. Undoubtedly, marketing activities should be carried under a well-thought out philosophy of efficient, effective, and socially responsible marketing. However, there are five competing concepts under which organizations conduct marketing activities: the production concept, selling concept, marketing concept, customer concept, and societal marketing concept.

The Production Concept

The production concept is one of the oldest concept in business. The production concept holds that consumers will prefer products that are widely available and inexpensive. Managers of production-oriented business concentrate on achieving high production efficiency, low costs, and mass distribution. They assume that consumers would be primarily interested in product availability and low prices. This orientation makes sense in developing countries, where consumers are more interested in obtaining the product than its features. It is also used when a company wants to expand the market. Some service organizations also operate on the production concept.

The Product Concept

Many businesses are guided by the product concept. The product concept holds that consumers will favor those products that offer the most quality, performance, or innovative features.

Managers in these organizations focus on making superior products and improving them over time. They assume that buyers admire well-made products and can appraise quality and performance. However, these managers are sometimes too attached with their product and do not realize what the market needs. Management might commit the "better-mousetrap" fallacy, believing that a better mousetrap will lead people to beat a path to its door.

The Selling Concept

The selling concept is another common business orientation. The selling concept holds that consumers and businesses, if left alone, will ordinarily not buy enough of the organizations products. The organization must, therefore, undertake an aggressive selling and promotion effort.

This has been the case with a large number of organizations in India. This concept assumes that consumers typically show buying inertia or resistance and must be coaxed into buying. It also assumes that the company has a whole battery of effective selling and promotion tools to stimulate more buying.

The Marketing Concept

The marketing concept is a business philosophy that challenges the three business orientations that have just been discussed. The marketing concept holds that the key to achieving its organizational goals consists of the company being more effective than competitors in creating, delivering, and communicating customer values to its chosen target markets. The marketing concept rests on four pillars: target market, customer needs, integrated marketing, and profitability. The selling concept takes an inside-out perspective. It starts with the factory, focuses on the existing products, and calls for heavy selling and promoting to produce profitable sales. The marketing concept takes an outside-in perspective. It starts with a well-defined market, focuses on customer needs, coordinates all the activities that will affect customers, and produces profits by satisfying customers.

- **Target market**
  Companies do best when they select their target markets carefully and prepare tailored marketing programs.
- **Customer needs**
  A company can define its target market but fail to correctly understand the customers' needs. Understanding customer needs and wants is not always simple. Some customers have needs of which they are not fully conscious or they cannot articulate these needs or they use words that require some interpretation. Needs can be distinguished on following five types:

1. Stated needs
2. Real needs
3. Unstated needs
4. Delight needs
5. Secret needs

Responding only to the stated need may really not work for the customer. The entire marketing effort would enable that.
- **Profitability**
  The ultimate purpose of the marketing concept is to help organizations achieve their objectives. In the case of private firms, the major objective is profit; in the case of nonprofit

and public organizations, it is surviving and attracting enough funds. A company makes money by satisfying customer needs better than its competitors. Most companies do not embrace the marketing concept until driven by circumstances. These are:

(a) Sales Decline: When sales fall, companies panic and look for answers.
(b) Slow Growth: Slow sales growth leads companies to search for new markets. They realize they need marketing skills to identify and select new opportunities.
(c) Changing buying patterns: Many companies operate in markets characterized by rapidly changing customer wants. These companies need more marketing know-how if they are to track buyers changing values.
(d) Increasing Competition: Complacent industries may be suddenly attacked by powerful competitors. Companies in deregulated industries all find it necessary to build up marketing expertise.
(e) Increasing Marketing Expenditures: Companies may find their expenditures for advertising, sales, promotion, marketing research and customer service to be poorly done. Management then decides to take a serious audit to improve its marketing.

Companies need to attract and retain customers through superior product offerings, which deliver the customer satisfaction. This is also influenced by other departments who must cooperate in delivering this customer satisfaction. In the course to converting into marketing orientation, a company faces three hurdles

1. Organized Resistance
2. Slow Learning
3. Fast forgetting

Some company departments like R&D, manufacturing, and finance believe a stronger marketing department threatens their power in the organization. Resistance is especially strong in the industries where marketing is introduced for the first time—like colleges, deregulated industries, and government offices. But in spite of resistance the company head may establish a marketing department, hire marketing talent, increase marketing budget and introduce marketing planning and control systems. Companies also often face a difficult task in adapting ad slogans to international markets, many of which are interpreted wrongly and erode value.

Integrated Marketing Concept

Integrated marketing is an approach when all the company's departments work together to serve the customer's interests, the result is integrated marketing. Unfortunately, not all employees are trained and motivated to work for the customer. Integrated marketing takes place on two levels. First, the various marketing functions—sales force, advertising, customer service, product management, marketing research—must work together. Second, the other departments must embrace marketing; they must also think like the customer. Marketing is not a department so much as a companywide orientation. To foster teamwork among all departments, a company should carry out internal as well as external marketing. External marketing is marketing directed at people outside the company. Internal marketing is the task of hiring, training, and motivating able employees who want to serve the customers well. In fact, internal marketing must precede external marketing. It makes no sense to promise excellent service before the company's staff is ready to provide it. Managers who believe the customer is the company's only true profit center consider the traditional organization chart—a pyramid with the president at the top, management in the middle, and front-line people and customers at the bottom—obsolete. Master marketing companies invert the chart.

Societal Marketing Concept

The societal marketing concept holds that the organization's task is to determine the needs, wants, and interests of target markets and to deliver the desired satisfaction more effectively and efficiently than competitors in a way that preserves and enhances the consumers and the societies well being. It calls for social and ethical considerations in marketing. They must balance the conflicting criteria of company profits, consumer want satisfaction, and public interest. In an age of environmental deterioration, resource shortage, explosive population growth, world hunger and poverty, and lack of social services, marketers need to be sensitive on these issues.

Thus it can be understood that at the firm level value has to be matched from two perspectives: firm and the customer. The task of any business is to deliver customer value at a profit. In a hypercompetitive market with increasing numbers of informed buyers faced with abundant choices, a company can win only by fine tuning the value delivery process and choosing, providing, and communicating superior value. For this the value delivery process also has to be understood.

The Value Delivery Process

The traditional view of marketing is that the firm makes a product and then sells it, with marketing taking place in the selling process. Companies that subscribe to this view have the best chance of succeeding in economies marked by goods shortages where consumers are not fussy about quality, features, or style. This traditional view will not work however in economies with very different type of people, each with different wants, perceptions, preferences, and buying criteria. The smart competitor must design and deliver offerings for well-defined target markets. This realization inspired a new wave of business processes that place marketing at the beginning of planning. Instead of emphasizing making and selling, companies now see themselves as the part of the value creation and delivery process. The value creation and delivery process can be divided into the following phases:

(a) Assessing market opportunities and customer value

This involves environment scanning and developing insights about customer needs, wants, and motives.

(b) Choosing the value

This includes critical decisions pertaining to segmenting, targeting, positioning, and branding.

(c) Designing the value

This relates to decisions involving products/service strategy, new offerings, and pricing

(d) Delivering value focuses on distribution and access issues

(e) Communicating value through integrated marketing communication choosing amongst various choices in the mass and personalized media.

Finally the value so created needs to be grown and sustained through globalization and holistic marketing organization. Thus the value creation and delivery process begins much before there is a product or service and continues through development and after the launch.

The Value Chain—An Aid in Creation and Delivery of Value

Michael Porter (1985) proposed the Value Chain as a tool for identifying ways to create more customer value. Every firm is a synthesis of activities performed to design, produce, market, deliver, and support its product. The value chain (Figure 1.2) identifies nine strategically relevant activities—five primary and four support activities—that create value and cost in a specific business. The primary activities are:

1.   Inbound Logistics, or bringing materials into business
2.   Operations, or converting materials into final products

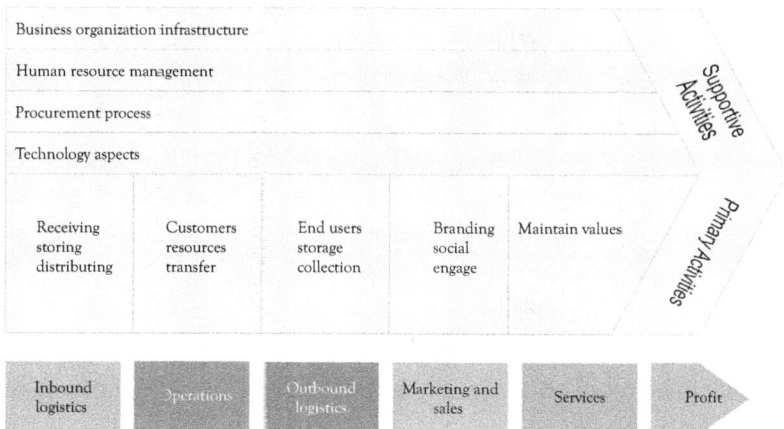

Figure 1.2 Value chain

3.   Outbound logistics, or shipping out final products
4.   Marketing, which includes sales
5.   Service.

Specialized departments that handle the support activities:

1.   Procurement
2.   Technology Development
3.   Human Resource Development
4.   Firm Infrastructure (Infrastructure covers the costs of general management, planning, finance, accounting, legal, and government affairs).

The firm's task is to examine its costs and performance in each value creating activity and look for ways to improve it. Managers should estimate competitor's costs and performances as benchmarks against which to compare their own. The firm's success depends on not how well each department performs its work, but also on how well the company coordinates departmental activities to conduct core business processes. These processes include:

- The market sensing process
- The new offering realizing process
- The customer acquisition process
- The customer relationship process
- The fulfillment management process

There have been adaptations to the value chain because of integration of technology but the concept remains the same. Since the concept has been sufficiently elaborated the further evolutions on the theory are not being detailed again.

Through the uniqueness in resources and activities across the value chain the firm may be able to build some core competencies which would help in differentiating its offer to the customer and thus creating roots of competitive advantage.

Value from the SD Logic Perspective

The most notable change in the marketing thought was the emergence of the services marketing thought. Webster argued in the early 1990s that, "the historical marketing management function based on the microeconomic maximization paradigm, must be critically examined for its relevance to marketing theory and practice." By the end of the year 2000 many marketing scholars started to gather for a new call to marketing that would consider relationship marketing, quality management, market orientation, supply and value chain management, resource management, and networks. The 4Ps became a handy framework but given the nature of network organization, their theoretical underpinnings and the impact that would be on the organization of consumption asked for an alternative paradigm in marketing that would consider all of the above and account for continuous nature of relationships amongst actors (Sheth and Parvathiyaar 1999; Achrol and Kotler 1999). Marketing at the turn of the millennium moved from the dominant logic focused on exchange of tangible goods (manufactured things) toward exchange of intangibles, that is, specialized skills and processes. Thus marketing became more inclusive.

Resources could be viewed as intangible and dynamic functions of human ingenuity and appraisal and not limited to a static stuff of Malthusian orientation, which considers natural resources through which human beings draw support and must be captured uniquely for an advantage. According to Vargo and Lusch the brains behind SD logic, Resource "become" when human kind knows what to do with it.

Constantin and Lusch 1994 define operand resources as resources on which an operation or act is performed to produce an effect, and they compare operand resources with operant resources, which are employed to act on operand resources (and other operant recourses). During most of civilization, human activity has been concerned largely with acting on the land, animal life, plant life, minerals, and other natural resources. Because these resources are finite, nations, clans, tribes, or other groups that possessed natural resources were considered wealthy. A goods-centered dominant logic developed in which the operand resources were considered primary. A firm (or nation) had factors of production (largely operand resources) and a technology (an operant resource), which had value to the extent that the firm could convert its operand resources into outputs at a low cost. Customers, like resources, became something to be captured or acted on, as English vocabulary would eventually suggest; we "segment" the market, "penetrate" the market, and "promote to" the market all in hope of attracting customers. Share of operand resources and share of (an operand) market was the key to success. Operant resources are resources that produce effects (Constantin and Lusch 1994). The relative role of operant resources began to shift in the late 20th century as humans began to realize that skills and knowledge were the most important types of resources. Zimmermann (1951) and Penrose (1959) were two of the first economists to recognize the shifting role and view of resources. As Hunt (2000) observes, Penrose did not use the popular term "factor of production" but rather used the term "collection of productive resources." Penrose suggested (pp. 24–25; emphasis in original) that "it is never resources themselves that are the 'inputs' to the production process, but only the services that the resources can render." Operant resources are often invisible and intangible; often they are core competences or organizational processes. They are likely to be dynamic and infinite and not static and finite, as is usually the case with operand resources. Because operant resources produce effects, they enable humans both to multiply the value of natural resources and to create additional operant resources. resources are not; they become (Zimmermann 1951). The service-centered dominant logic perceives operant resources as primary, because they are the producers of effects. This shift in the primacy of resources has implications for how exchange processes, markets, and customers are perceived and approached.

The classification of development of the services marketing thought is also based on this orientation. With the changed worldview the classification in marketing literature becomes irrelevant to the extent that countries without an advantage in operand resources may still be powerful both in demand and supply based on their advantages in operant resources such as skilled labor for which India is a good example. The table above shows the different schools of thought in marketing where there is a fundamental difference in the view of conceptualization of value. The service-centered view of marketing implies that marketing is a continuous series of social and economic processes that is largely focused on operant resources with which the firm is constantly striving to make better value propositions than its competitors. In a free enterprise system, the firm primarily knows whether it is making better value propositions from the feedback it receives from the marketplace in terms of firm financial performance. Because firms can always do better at serving customers and improving financial performance, the service-centered view of marketing perceives marketing as a continuous learning process (directed at improving operant resources). The service-centered view can be stated as follows:

1. Identify or develop core competences, the fundamental knowledge and skills of an economic entity that represent potential competitive advantage.
2. Identify other entities (potential customers) that could benefit from these competences.
3. Cultivate relationships that involve the customers in developing customized, competitively compelling value propositions to meet specific needs.
4. Gauge marketplace feedback by analyzing financial performance from exchange to learn how to improve the firm's offering to customers and improve firm performance.

This view is grounded in and largely consistent with resource advantage theory (Conner and Prahalad 1996; Hunt 2000; Srivastava, Fahey, and Christensen 2001) and core competency theory (Day 1994; Prahalad and Hamel 1990). Core competences are not physical assets but intangible processes; they are "bundles of skills and technologies" (Hamel and Prahalad 1994, p. 202) and are often routines, actions, or operations that are tacit, causally ambiguous, and idiosyncratic (Nelson and Winter 1982; Polanyi 1966). Hunt (2000, p. 24) refers to core competences as higher-order resources because they are bundles of basic resources. Teece and Pisano (1994, p. 537) suggest that "the competitive advantage of firms stems from dynamic capabilities rooted in high performance routines operating inside the firm, embedded in the firm's processes, and conditioned by its history." Hamel and Prahalad (p. 202; 204) discuss "competition for competence," or competitive advantage resulting from competence making a "disproportionate contribution to customer-perceived value." The focus of marketing on core competences inherently places marketing at the center of the integration of business functions and disciplines. As Prahalad and Hamel (1990, p. 82) suggest, "core competence is communication, involvement, and a deep commitment to working across organizational boundaries." In addition, they state that core competences are "collective learning in the organization, especially about how to coordinate diverse production skills." This cross-functional, intraorganizational boundary spanning also applies to the interorganizational boundaries of vertical marketing systems or networks. Channel intermediaries and network partners represent core competences that are organized to gain competitive advantage by performing specialized marketing functions. The firms can have long-term viability only if they learn in conjunction with and are coordinated with other channel and network partners. This is a more value aligned view to Marketing. The service-centered view of marketing is customercentric (Sheth, Sisodia, and Sharma 2000) and market driven (Day 1999). This means more than simply being consumer oriented; it means collaborating with and learning from customers and being adaptive to their individual and dynamic needs. A service-centered dominant logic implies that value is defined by and cocreated with the consumer rather than embedded in output. Haeckel (1999) observes successful firms moving from practicing a "make-and-sell" strategy to a "sense-and-respond" strategy. Day (1999) argues for thinking in terms of self-reinforcing "value cycles" rather than linear value chains. In the service-centered view of marketing, firms are in a process of continual hypothesis generation and testing. Outcomes (for example, financial) are not something to be maximized but something to learn from as firms try to serve customers better and improve their performance. Thus, a market-oriented and learning organization (Slater and Narver 1995) is compatible with, if not implied by, the service-centered model. Because of its central focus on dynamic and learned core competences, the emerging service-centered dominant logic is also compatible with emerging theories of the firm. For example, Teece and Pisano (1994, p. 540) emphasize that competences and capabilities are "ways of organizing and getting things done, which cannot be accomplished by using the price system to coordinate activity." Having described the goods- and service-centered views of marketing, we turn to ways that the views are different. Six differences between the goods- and service-centered dominant logic, all centered on the distinction between operand and operant resources, are presented in Table 1.1. The six attributes and our eight foundational premises (FPs) (Table 1.2) help present the patchwork of the emerging dominant logic.

Table 1.1 *Differences between goods and services centered logic*

	Goods-centered dominant logic	Service-centered dominant logic
Primary unit of exchange	People exchange for goods. These goods serve as operand resources	People exchange to acquire the benefits of specialized competencies (knowledge and skills), or services. Knowledge and skills are operant resources
Role of goods	Goods are operand resources and end products. Marketers take matter and change its form, place, time, and possession	Goods are transmitters of operant resources (embedded knowledge); they are intermediate products that are used by other operant resources as appliances in value creation process
Role of customer	The customer is the recipient of goods. Marketers do things to customers, they segment them, penetrate them, distribute and promote to them. The customer is an operand resource	The customer is a co-producer of service. Marketing is a process of doing things in interaction with the customer. The customer is primarily an operant resource, only functioning occasionally as an operand resource
Determination and meaning of value	Value is determined by the producer. It is embedded in the operand resource and is defined in terms of exchange value	Value is perceived and determined by the consumer on the basis of value in use. Value results from the beneficial application of operant resources sometimes transmitted through operand resources. Firms can only make value propositions
Firm–customer interaction	The customer is an operand resource. Customers are acted on to create transactions with resources	The customer is primarily an operant resource. Customers are active participants in relational exchanges and coproduction
Sources of economic growth	Wealth is obtained from surplus tangible resources and goods. Wealth consists of owning, controlling, and producing operand resources	Wealth is obtained through the application and exchange of specialized knowledge and skills. It represents the right to the future use of operant resource

Source: Vargo, S.L., and R.F. Lusch. January 2004. "Evolving to a New Dominant Logic for Marketing." *Journal of Marketing* 68, pp. 1–17. Vargo, S.L., and R.F. Lusch. Spring 2008. "Service-Dominant Logic: Continuing the Evolution." *Journal of the Academy of Marketing Science* 36, pp. 1-10, Vargo, S.L., and R.F. Lusch. 2016. "Institutions and Axioms: An Extension and Update of Service-Dominant Logic." *Journal of the Academy of Marketing Science*, pp. 1–19.

Table 1.2 Service-dominant logic axioms and foundational premises

Axiom 1/FP1	Service is the fundamental basis of exchange
FP2	Indirect exchange masks the fundamental basis of exchange
FP3	Goods are a distribution mechanism for service provision
FP4	Operant resources are the fundamental source of strategic benefit
FP5	All economies are service economies
Axiom 2/FP6	Value is cocreated by multiple actors, always including the beneficiary
FP7	Actors cannot deliver value but can participate in the creation and offering of value propositions
FP8	A service-centered view is inherently customer oriented and relational
Axiom 3/FP9	All social and economic actors are resource integrators
Axiom 4/FP10	Value is always uniquely and phenomenologically determined by the beneficiary
Axiom 5/FP11	Value cocreation is coordinated through actor-generated institutions and institutional arrangements

Source: Vargo, S.L., and R.F. Lusch. January 2004. "Evolving to a New Dominant Logic for Marketing." *Journal of Marketing* 68, pp. 1–17. Vargo, S.L., and R.F. Lusch. Spring 2008. "Service-Dominant Logic: Continuing the Evolution." *Journal of the Academy of Marketing Science* 36, pp. 1–10, Vargo, S.L., and R.F. Lusch. 2016. "Institutions and Axioms: an Extension and Update of Service-Dominant Logic." *Journal of the Academy of Marketing Science*, pp. 1–19.

Customer Perceived Value (CPV)

It is important for marketers to understand how customers make choices. Customers tend to be value maximizers within the bounds of search costs and limited knowledge, mobility, and income. Customers estimate which offer they believe for whatever reason will deliver the most perceived value and act on it. Whether the offer lives up to the expectations affects customer satisfaction and the probability that the customer will purchase the product again. CPV is the difference between the prospective customer's evaluation of all the benefits and costs of an offering and the perceived alternatives. Total customer benefit is the perceived monetary value of the bundle of economic, functional, and psychological benefits customers expect from a given product offering because of the product, service, people, and image. Total customer cost is the perceived bundle of costs customers expect to incur in evaluating, obtaining, using, and disposing of the market offering, including monetary, time, energy, and psychological costs. CPV thus is based on the difference between the benefits the customer gets and the costs assumed for different choices. The marketer can increase the value of the customer offering by raising economic, functional, or emotional benefits and reducing the associated costs.

The Indian BOP Context

Since the start of the millennium, many scholars have started exploring the Base of the Pyramid (BOP) market, *for example,* Prahlad and Hart 2002; Guesalaga and Marshall 2008; Ireland 2008; Sheth 2011; Kolk et al. 2014, and so on, and advocated the view that marketing was perhaps the best way to develop such market and to generate corporate profits as it was advantageous in terms of both scale and scope. The BOP segment in India has been estimated to be a USD 1.2 trillion market, out of a global USD 5 trillion (WRI. However, in order to realize the potential, multinational companies would have to redesign the business models, products, and services for the necessary value improvement and cost reduction (Ireland 2008). *A sound understanding of BOP consumers and their purchase behavior* would be the prerequisite for the market development and subsequent demand fulfillment (Guesalaga and Marshall 2008; Ireland 2008; Sheth 2011; Kolk et al. 2014). There has been an increase in the research interest in BOP from marketing researchers in developed countries as well as the emerging economies since 2001 (Singh and Bhardwaj 2017). A basic search on Ebscohost on the keywords "Bottom of the Pyramid/Base of the Pyramid" returned 5,658 articles of which only 92 were in the consumer behavior domain of which only 9 were from India. The BOP research has been built in contexts around subsistence and poverty related to consumption and transformative marketing, yet *Marketing as a discipline needs to address this segment of consumers in their own right and work around solutions to provide them value.* This momentum needs to be build and there is a need for studying and understanding the customer here as they are embedded in a different sociocultural context.

The BOP segments are constrained by their disposable income; of the four billion living at the BOP, 1.4 billion have daily incomes of between $2 and $8, and 2.6 billion of them earn <$2 per day (Hammond et al. 2007; UNDP 2008). In India, 469million people earn $1.25 per day and 850 million people earn $2 per day (The World Bank 2014). The aggregated purchasing power of the BOP people in India represents more than $1 trillion, while the global figure is more than $5 trillion (Hammond et al. 2007). The majority of the BOP population in India lives in rural areas (Hammond et al. 2007). The poor infrastructure makes transportation from and to these villages difficult. As a result, poor people lack easy access to more competitive markets (Vachani and Smith 2008). The majority of poor people are illiterate, which constrains their decision making; according to the 2013/2014 Education for All Global Monitoring Report published by UNESCO (2014), India has the highest population of illiterate adults at 287 million. These characteristics of the BOP markets have several implications for the MNCs targeting it. Studies have revealed that companies cannot apply their traditional marketing strategies, such as advertising in television and magazines, due to BOP people's illiteracy and lack of access to such media (London et al. 2010; Prahalad 2010). Traditional distribution channels cannot be employed at the BOP due to the insufficient physical infrastructure. When MNCs target this market, they cannot rely on their own existing knowledge based on developed markets, and have to devise innovative solutions. Some scholars argue that innovation at the BOP should be built around the four A's of Awareness, Acceptability, Affordability, and Availability of products (Anderson and Billou 2007); MNCs have to build awareness about the product, make sure that low-income people accept the benefits of using it, ensure its affordability and make it available in remote areas (Anderson and Billou 2007). Knowledge and behavior can differ across these markets.

Customer Perceived Value and Urban India BOP Customer

One of the most important tasks in marketing has been to create and communicate value to customers to drive their satisfaction, loyalty, and profitability. The subject of CPV has been dealt repeatedly in the marketing literature starting from unidimensional conceptualization that was fairly simpler to assess, moving to the multidimensional concept that was thought to be richer as it considered the emotional dimensions along with economic and cognitive ones and further on to the measurement, which has been highly conflicting. CPV is the customer's net valuation of the perceived benefits accrued from an offering that is based on the costs that they are willing to give up for the needs that are seeking to satisfy (Kumar and Reinartz 2016). *However, the majority of research on CPV assumes that value perceptions affect all buyers equally. Few studies have examined consumer heterogeneity in relation to value* (Ruiz, Castro, and Armario 2007, Floh, Zauner, Koller, and Rusch 2014), *and its explanatory power regarding behavioral intentions.* An aggregate analysis of CPV, disregarding heterogeneous consumer preferences (sub-populations), might result in misleading parameter estimates and inferior managing decisions (Desarbo et al. 2001). One of the key characteristics of Emerging Markets such as India is heterogeneity. In PPP terms, the Indian BOP market contributed to about 85 percent of the total national household market of which *22 percent is the Urban BOP, which may be referred as to the next billion,* that is, where the immediate opportunity lies for the organized businesses but the individual in this segment has not been studied. This segment is already in the business vicinity and reach, has aspirations, and profit realization may happen in relatively short term that could be sustained over long term if the segment is satisfied.

Detailed discussion on CPV has been done in Chapter 3 through the ways it has been dealt in literature and the context of BOP.

Emerging Markets, Value, and BOP

Defining Emerging Markets

Historically several perspectives have been used to define and describe emerging markets. Two of the more commonly employed perspectives are first a financial growth perspective, and second an economic levels perspective.

Financial Growth Perspective

Financial institutions focused on financial growth characteristics to identify emerging markets for both the benefit of their clients, and as a basis for their own competitive advantage in the financial industry. Investment and stock equity portfolios were created to capitalize on the expected growth in these emerging markets. The historical sequence of the Financial Growth perspective in emerging market groupings is presented below:

- BRICs—In 2001, Jim O'Neill of Goldman Sachs, identified and labeled the four largest emerging markets with the fastest growing GDPs as the BRIC countries—Brazil, Russia, India, and China (O'Neill 2001). The BRIC countries were identified as the economic growth opportunities of the future with the potential for substantial future development.
- Next 11—In late 2005, Goldman Sachs identified and labeled the next set of large-population countries beyond the BRICs as the Next 11 countries—Bangladesh, Egypt, Indonesia, Iran, Korea, Mexico, Nigeria, Pakistan, Philippines, Turkey, and Vietnam (Wilson and Stupnytska 2007). The Next 11 were identified as a secondary pool of emerging markets.
- BRICS—As a result of the tremendous interest in the innovative BRIC acronym, the four BRIC countries began to engage in joint economic development activities. In 2006 the BRIC foreign ministers met in New York, with the first annual BRIC Summit taking place in Russia in 2009 (Kramer 2009). In 2010, South Africa was invited to attend the annual BRIC Summit as a guest member, and at the 2011 BRIC Summit South Africa formally joined, establishing the BRICS grouping.
- CIVETS—In 2009, Robert Ward of The Economist Intelligence Unit identified six emerging market countries with large and young populations, diversified economies, relative political stability, and decent financial systems: Colombia, Indonesia, Vietnam, Egypt, Turkey, and South Africa (Economist 2009).
- EAGLEs—In November 2010, Banco Bilbao Vizcaya Argentaria, S.A. (BBVA), the second largest bank in Spain, created the Emerging and Growth-Leading Economies (EAGLEs). EAGLEs were selected as those countries expected to contribute more to global GDP growth than the average of the six largest developed economies (excluding the United States)

each year for the next ten years (GarciaHerrero, Navia, and Nigrinis 2010). The initial ten EAGLEs included: Brazil, Russia, India, China, Egypt, Indonesia, South Korea, Mexico, Taiwan, and Turkey.

- MIST—In January 2011, Jim O'Neill of Goldman Sachs presented a new tier of large rapidly growing emerging economies called MIST countries: Mexico, Indonesia, South Korea, and Turkey (Gupta 2011). The MIST countries shared the three common traits: a large population and market, a big economy with each ~1 percent of global GDP, and membership in the G20.

- MINT—In May 2011, Fidelity International identified new emerging market investment opportunities, which it labeled the MINT countries: Mexico, Indonesia, Nigeria, and Turkey (Bamford 2011).

Economic Levels Perspective

Economists adopted a different methodology, initially focusing on classifying the economic levels of emerging markets. Hoskisson, Eden, Lau, and Wright (2000) identified emerging economies as low income, rapid-growth countries using economic liberalization as their primary engine of growth. Hoskisson et al. (2000) divided these emerging economies into two major categories: (1) developing countries as found in Asia, Latin America, Africa, and the Middle East, and (2) transition economies as found in the former Soviet Union and China.

India by both financial and economic perspective has been classified as an Emerging Market with a big BOP population. At this stage it seems pertinent to see the evolution of the BOP concept in literature

Evolution of the Bottom of the Pyramid Concept

The First-Generation BOP

Prahalad and Hart (2002) observed that MNCs were realizing neither the expected product sales nor the resulting financial and marketing benefits from the identified middle-class emerging markets. Prahalad and Hart stated that the "prospect of millions of 'middle class' consumers in developing countries, clamoring for products from MNCs, was wildly oversold" (2002, p. 1). The authors proposed that the MNCs had incorrectly focused on middle-class consumers, when they should have focused on "the billions of aspiring poor who are joining the market economy for the first time" (2002, p. 1). In defining the economic levels of the BOP market, Prahalad utilized the framework of the WEP. Prahalad utilized the economic measure of Purchasing Power Parity (PPP) to compare the economic states of multiple countries (Prahalad 2005; Prahalad and Hammond 2002). Prahalad's early conceptualizations of the BOP progressed through several iterations, ultimately solidifying into a conceptual structure with five tiers of economic income levels (Prahalad 2005; Prahalad and Hammond 2002; Prahalad and Hart 2002).

- Tier 1: At the top of the WEP were 75 to 100 million affluent global consumers (1.7 percent of the global population) predominantly in the developed countries, with an annual income level greater than $20,000 in PPP.
- Tier 2 and Tier 3: These two tiers represent 1.5 to 1.75 billion people (29.9 percent): poor consumers in developed nations and the rising middle class in developing countries, with an annual income level of $1,500 to $20,000 in PPP.
- Tier 4 and Tier 5: The bottom of the WEP represents 4.0 billion people (68.4 percent) at literally the bottom of the pyramid: poor consumers in developing countries, with an annual income level of less than $1,500 in PPP.

Core Benefits of the BOP Approach

Prahalad and Hart (2002) proposed two core benefits. First, the benefits to the MNCs included substantially increased product sales growth and revenues. The increases in revenues were attributed to improved operating efficiencies, the use of technologies, and the identification of new sources of innovation (Hammond and Prahalad 2004; Prahalad and Hammond 2002). Second, the potential for global poverty alleviation was identified as an obtainable goal. Prahalad's approach was based on "doing well" financially, while simultaneously "doing good" for those in the BOP (Prahalad and Hammond 2002).

The Second-Generation BOP

In 2006, the World Resources Institute (WRI) and the International Finance Corporation (IFC) released an in-depth comprehensive study of the world's socioeconomic structure (Hammond et al. 2007; World Resources Institute 2006). The WRI and the IFC examined aggregate data in four developing regions—Africa, Asia, Eastern Europe, and Latin America with the Caribbean; they examined 110 countries for which household data was available. This resulted in three population segments.

- The Top of the Pyramid: the high-income population segment contained annual incomes above $20,000 (in 2002 PPP).
- The Middle of the Pyramid: the mid-market population segment contained annual incomes above $3,000 and up to and including $20,000 (in 2002 PPP).
- The BOP: The BOP population segment was defined as those annual incomes up to and including $3,000 (in 2002 PPP). Extending the initial Prahalad model, London and Hart (2011) defined a second generation of approaches with both evolutionary orientations and value propositions. This second-generation approach defined a fortune creating perspective with an emphasis on cocreating new business models, technology solutions, and value propositions with the BOP (London and Hart 2011).

Opposing Views Challenging the BOP Perspective

While beyond the scope of this book to resolve challenges to the BOP approach, these differing perspectives are recognized. First, the existence of a BOP market opportunity is foundationally based on the capability of the people in the BOP to be consumers of products (Prahalad and Hart 2002). The fundamental existence of this potential for BOP consumption faced ongoing challenges from several authors (Karnani 2007;

Walsh, Kress, and Beyerchen 2005). The BOP market opportunity based on BOP consumption received the strongest challenge from Karnani, who utilized an economic perspective to directly challenge Prahalad's belief that consumption in the BOP market could effectively alleviate poverty, stating "their problem is that they cannot afford to consume more" (Karnani 2007). Second, Karnani also challenged Prahalad's estimation of the size of the BOP market opportunity, stating "not only is the BOP market quite small, it is unlikely to be very profitable, especially for a large company" (Karnani 2007). Karnani attributed the lack of profitability to multiple factors, including (1) an initial overestimation of the size of the BOP market and (2) the high marketing and distribution costs associated with serving the poor who are geographically dispersed. Third, BOP marketing has been recognized since its inception as an instrumental process for driving poverty alleviation on a global basis, described as "lifting billions of people out of poverty and desperation" (Prahalad and Hart 2002). BOP for poverty alleviation again received its strongest challenge from Karnani, who raised both political-philosophical and economic challenges to Prahalad's BOP approach for poverty alleviation. Karnani labeled Prahalad's BOP approach as a libertarian model which proposed that free markets reduce poverty (2008b, 2008c, 2010). Karnani's political-philosophical viewpoint had fundamental criticisms of Prahalad's BOP approach: (1) there was too little emphasis on the legal, social, and regulatory mechanisms to protect the vulnerable poor consumers, and (2) there was an over-emphasis on microcredit, and an under-emphasis on creating employment opportunities (Karnani 2008a, 2008c, 2008d, 2010). And finally, a viewpoint supporting the status quo of existing business models was raised by Garrette and Karnani (2010) who examined three case studies, and concluded that while the context in BOP markets is different from the context found in well-developed markets, the existing business principles continue to be an effective guide to strategy development in a BOP market.

Distinct Characteristics of the BOP Market

Early research identified BOP markets as possessing unique characteristics, specifically existing as non-homogeneous market segments both within and across countries (London 2007). With increasing awareness of the BOP market as a potentially attractive and viable market, marketers seeking a competitive advantage BOP market and the superior financial performance that accompanies that competitive advantage began to study the BOP market. Kennedy and Novogratz (2011) identified five unique factors that describe the BOP markets: (1) There are many unaddressed needs at the BOP, both government provided and those neglected needs because people are perceived to be too poor. (2) BOP markets are beset by poor infrastructure with inadequate distribution networks and poor access to both education and information. (3) Corruption is common, sapping economic value from the system. (4) Low purchasing power makes it difficult for new goods and services to enter the market. (5) There is a lack of equity capital, as traditional capital providers typically bypass BOP entrepreneurs.

Marketing to the BOP

To successfully introduce goods and services into BOP markets, traditional marketing theories will need to be validated for applicability. With the articulation of the WEP framework and the recognition of the inherent bias of the MNCs in their strategic approach to the BOP market, Prahalad proposed an alternative to the traditional 4Ps: the 4As (Prahalad 2005; 2012). His 4As include:

1. Awareness of the product and service so that the BOP consumer knows what is available, and how to use the product or service.
2. Affordability of the product or service for the BOP consumer.
3. Access to the product or service, even for those consumers in remote geographical areas.
4. Availability of the product or service with an uninterrupted or continuous supply of the product or service.

Strategic Approaches to BOP Markets

Topics that have received substantial focus in the BOP literature are management strategy, strategic development, and strategic approaches for doing business in the BOP markets. Ricart, Enright, Ghemawat, Hart, and Khanna (2004) found that the BOP highlighted significant limitations in the approaches to global and emerging market strategies; these authors found that attempts to leverage existing MNC capabilities are inadequate in entering BOP markets.

New Capabilities and New Business Models

The BOP requirement for new MNC capabilities has been identified by multiple studies. Seelos and Mair (2007) reviewed the initial BOP strategic literature identifying the requirement to develop new capabilities and business models to foster marketing success in BOP markets. Olsen and Boxenbaum found that the BOP market requires the development of new business approaches "related to buying, manufacturing, packaging, marketing, distributing and advertising products" (2009). Wright, Filatotchev, Hoskisson, and Peng (2005) identified four new market entry strategies and introduced a strategic framework employing two categories of markets: well-developed and emerging markets. The four market entry strategies include: (1) firms from developed economies entering emerging economies, (2) domestic emerging market firms competing within their own emerging market, (3) emerging market firms entering other emerging markets, and (4) emerging market firms entering developed economies.

Thus based on the above discussion it becomes evident that BOP is a strong segment that cannot be ignored by management practitioners and academicians in the emerging markets context such as India. The subsequent chapters would highlight how marketing needs to identify and address CPV at the Urban BOP in India closing with a long-term institutionalizing strategy. Before closing on this chapter building on multiple perspectives of value it is important to touch upon South Africa which is very similar to India as an Emerging Market and has a big BOP population. This section highlights certain key points related to the way research has looked at the BOP concept in South Africa.

BOP and South Africa

Studies in countries such as Brazil have concentrated on the company's strategies to meet the BOP market needs (Giovinazzo 2003, Spers and Wright 2006, and Spers 2007). These studies show that companies concentrating on BOP have obtained better results, in terms of growth, profits, and operational results, than those companies focusing on social classes of higher income groups. Spers and Wright (2015), however, specifically point out that it also becomes relevant to know the BOP needs, as consumers and also as producers. The authors subsequently have studied and presented the consumption characteristics of the BOP population in Brazil. The BOP population in Brazil accounts for 88 percent of the Brazilian population. The authors suggest that in such a case attention should be given to the consumption of popular and essential goods to meet the demands of low-income market. Cobra (2009) states that the popular class purchases, primarily for survival, while the upper class purchases also to boast the luxury. Housing and food captures most of this population income, followed by energy and transport (Spers and Wright 2015). As suggested by Vaz (2006) the consumers with low purchasing power are seen, generally, as people who do not have money to spend and therefore appreciate lower prices, second-tier brands and are dependent on credit plans systems. However, considering this market size, the lower classes represent a significant purchasing power that is waiting to be explored in Brazil. The BOP represents a large share of Brazilian society that, despite having a restricted budget, is increasingly exposed to the advertising, publicity, and influences that awaken the consumption desire and has available income to choose what to purchase, being the price, although important, only one of the attributes to be analyzed in the purchasing process. The authors also note that although relevant, price is not the only determinant factor in the purchasing process of popular class: The stores and products need to be attractive, stylish and these income range customers must be treated with respect and, in addition, these popular consumers' desires and needs must be satisfied, which is not always reflected by what is cheaper and required for survival. According to Prahalad (2005), the consumption capacity creation is based on three basic principles: Purchasing power, access, and availability of goods/services. The author also states that the BOP population is highly brand aware. And it is also extremely conscious about value, considering the necessity and the impossibility of repurchasing. According to research by BCG (2002), the price has a weight of 31 percent to 38 percent on the purchase decision, according to the product category. But despite the price being relevant, this group has increasingly been trying to project its quest for social status in products that class A/B consumes as well as looking for quality in the purchased goods and services. The authors consider that the low-income consumers have the need for social inclusion, as opposed to the upper classes consumers, who want to be unique. Poorer consumers feel excluded from society; living in the fringes of society they feel inferior. The consumption, in turn, offers a sense of belonging in the group, is a way to feel as a part of society. To consume is good for self-esteem of such consumers (Oliveira 2006). The research concluded that the BOP population hardly saves or invests, it consumes, spending much of their income on consumer goods, whether they are essential or not. It is worth noting that this behavior is closely related to the income restriction, but also to the concept of belonging to a social group, and to the BOP population. Consumption is a way of social inclusion, makes the consumer feel as an integral part of society. Consuming is good for such consumer self esteem.

Most of the research papers in the context of value at the BOP have concentrated on corporate social entrepreneurship and creation of social value as the theme. This is relevant in making a real difference in the Urban Context in India as well. Ghauri, Tasavori, and Zaefarian 2014 have used the social entrepreneurship theory and network theory because social problems, such as poverty may be potential opportunities (Grayson and Hodges 2004). MNCs can employ socially entrepreneurial solutions at the BOP (Tasavori and Sinkovics 2010) and be referred to as corporate social entrepreneurs (Austin et al. 2008; Kuratko et al. 2011).

Social Entrepreneurship Theory and Corporate Social Entrepreneurship for Value Creation

Social entrepreneurs are those individuals who pursue the goal of social value creation where "social value creation has little to do with profits but instead involves the fulfillment of basic and long standing needs such as providing food, water, shelter, education and medical services to those members of society who are in need." To define the concept of social entrepreneurship and distinguish it from commercial entrepreneurship, Santos (2012, p. 337) employs economic theories and the concept of value, the latter being defined in terms of the "increase in the utility of society's members." According to Santos (2012), the difference between social entrepreneurship and commercial entrepreneurship is related to social value creation and value capturing. Social value creation occurs "when the aggregate utility of society's members increases after accounting for the opportunity cost of all the resources used in that activity." Value capture from an activity happens when the focal actor is able to appropriate a portion of the value created by the activity after accounting for the cost of resources that he/she mobilized (Santos 2012, p. 237). Based on these definitions, social value creation is measured at the societal level and value capture at the organizational level. It should be noted that, if organizations tend to succeed in capturing value (gaining profit), they have to offer social value creation. Commercial companies have to consider both social value creation and value capturing, and make a trade-off between them (Mizik and Jacobson 2003). How companies balance their value capturing and social value creation will affect how they are perceived by their stakeholders and customers. MNCs usually have the core aim of maximizing value capture and just satisfying social value creation by obeying laws and embarking on socially responsible activities. On the other hand, social entrepreneurs and NGOs usually pursue the maximization of social value creation, and capture value only as needed to sustain their activities. In addition, some activities that create value for society may not allow value to be captured. For example, in the context of the BOP, companies may not be able to capture value because of people' slow incomes and their inability to pay even if they want to (Seelos and Mair 2005). This is where social entrepreneurs come to the fore. They set the prices of their products and services in such a way that maximizes the utility for their customers. In contrast, commercial companies that are focused on value capturing will tend to set their prices at a level that maximizes their own profit. According to Santos (2012, p. 342) social entrepreneurs are involved in areas with strong positive externalities, "where the potential for value capture is lower than the potential for social value creation because the benefits for society of the activity go much beyond the benefits accrued to the entrepreneurs." Building upon this understanding, Santos (2012, pp. 341–47) offers a theory of social entrepreneurship that has four building blocks: (1) Social entrepreneurship involves addressing neglected problems in a society and creating positive externalities. These problems are usually ignored by the private sector and the government and, when addressed, they create value and benefit society. (2) Social entrepreneurship focuses on positive externalities whose benefits are both localized and favor less powerful segments of the population. (3) Social entrepreneurs aim to offer sustainable solutions to social problems. Sustainable solutions are methods that either permanently remove the key causes of the problem or develop a system to solve the problem on an ongoing basis. (4) Social entrepreneurs develop solutions based on empowerment logic. They endeavor to empower actors and entities (for example, beneficiaries, users, or partners) beyond organizational boundaries. Empowerment is the "process of increasing the assets and capabilities of individuals or groups to make purposive choices and to transform those choices into desired actions and outcomes" (World Bank 2009). The theme of social entrepreneurship if clubbed with the network theory of organizations forms a new entry mechanism for MNC wanting to enter Emerging markets. The extant literature suggests that successful entry into the BOP requires the establishment of relationships with NGOs (for example, Perez-Aleman and Sandilands 2008; Teegen 2006; Reficco and Márquez 2012; London and Hart 2004; Tasavori et al. 2014). Prior studies have revealed that collaborative relationships with NGOs can enable MNCs to get access to different resources, that other for-profit companies may lack or their internal development may take a long time (Teegen et al. 2004; Rondinelli and London 2003). The importance of NGOs' resource contribution are more critical at the BOP as the required resources are not available for purchase (Madhok 2000). To analyze the collaboration of MNCs with NGOs, and specifically the NGOs' activities and resources that can facilitate entry of MNCs into the BOP markets, we adopt the actors, resources, and activities framework (Elg et al. 2008; Ghauri et al. 2008; Hakansson and Snehota 1995). In a network relationship, the actors exchange and combine their resources through various activities for their mutual benefit. The actor dimension in this research comprises the MNCs and NGOs, the activities are those tasks that take place in order to facilitate collaboration, and the resources are associated with what the MNCs and NGOs bring to the table to facilitate their collaboration at the BOP.

Defining Urban BOP in India

For the purpose of this book we take the Boston Analytics (2012) definition for Urban BOP as per the following guidelines:

- The "Bottom of the Pyramid" (BOP) constitutes ~70 percent of India's total population (880 million); it has a combined disposable income of ~$358 billion.
- A large part of this population resides in the rural areas, estimates suggest that 78 percent of the BOP segment is composed of rural population, rest 22 percent being urban India, which would mean close to 200 million in population and a combined disposable income of ~$80 billion.

Conclusion

As may be seen through the chapter the different perspectives on value and its evolution in marketing need to be aligned by putting all the frames together against an anchor which is the context. The chapter closes by defining the context as to what constitutes Urban Bottom of the Pyramid in India.

CHAPTER 2

Customer Perceived Value and Its Drivers in Urban BOP in India

Introduction

In Chapter 1, the concept of value has been looked in detail through multiple perspectives: firm level and customer level, different marketing approaches, traditional and service-dominant one, and from different contexts including bottom of the pyramid in emerging markets mainly India and South Africa. Talking about urban India it is worthwhile to first understand and relate to the lives of the BOP customers and define as to what would constitute value for them. The following case illustrations will help us do this. Next an attempt has been made through qualitative research using grounded theory to understand how they make a purchase across product categories, what gives them happiness and satisfaction and what drives their expectations. The findings bear relevance and importance for marketers in India across product categories.

Sonu Singh, 36 Years, Auto Rickshaw Driver

Every day when Sonu got up in the morning he dreamt of closing his day big; big as big as may be INR 1,500–2,000 from the income from his passengers that would ride his auto on that day. At a dollar exchange price of 69.45 in a USD, this came to about USD 20–30 per day. But this is what he aspires whereas on an average he closes at about INR 750–1,000 per day for 25 days in a month. This was approximately USD 4$ per day. His family comprised of his wife and him. More than 90 percent of this income went in purchasing grocery, fruits and vegetables and around 10 percent was left for other needs of the family.

The glaze of the sparkling sun was broken by the shadow of his wife Devi who stood between the sun and him to bring him back to the reality from his dream, lying in the small portion outside his one room temporary shelter in the Silokhera slum of Gurugram city in Haryana. Standing with a cup of tea; the cup and saucer chipped, which were purchased from a kabariwala at a good bargain she was irritated. It was 7:30 a.m. in the morning and her husband was still lying dreaming in the bed. The early morning was the time for school traffic to peak. She was wondering how many passengers Sonu would have already missed because of his laziness, from a group of teachers, students, and parents who would have hired him for commuting between home and school. Their neighbor Munna had left the home at 6:30 a.m. already. She was worried that the INR 500 which her husband had lost in sleeping in a hour would have helped her purchase branded packaged atta which everybody was talking about in the town. Sharing her concern and reprimanding Sonu, she asked him to quickly get ready otherwise they would not be able to purchase the healthy Patanjali brand wheat flour. Sonu told her not to worry and continue with the purchase if the brand was so good. He asked her not to worry even if he did not make INR 1,500 that day which she was wishing for. Getting up to get ready Sonu told his wife to always consider the best purchase if health was the concern. He then went to freshen himself leaving his wife wondering if he could practically do this in the monthly income of INR 25,000 per month of which INR 4,000 went straight toward payment of room rent and electricity expenses combined to the landlord. The landlord collected similar rents from the hundred plus families that were living in the hundred rooms constructed in a plot size of one acre. Sonu was particularly perturbed that because of his earning capability his wife could not purchase which was otherwise the most prudent choice for the product. Talking to a fellow passenger who travelled with him every day he told, "what about us, how do we matter to anyone, there is a healthy atta brand but the prices are kept at a level that people like us cannot afford. What it means is that people's health and product options are linked to his income level whereas health is every individual's concern. Should we be denied this because we don't have money or should government and business become more sensitive and responsible to meet our needs." In the evening while returning home Sonu stopped at the neighborhood kirana store and purchased the 10 kg Patanjali atta brand for INR 320. He had earned INR 1,000 that day and also paid a challan of INR 600 for wrong side driving. The purchase made him extremely satisfied. After all he and his family were no less important than the people who earned better than him and he was also equal to them in terms of shouldering the family responsibilities. Devi did not ask for the INR 80 left with him as it would accommodate for his daily pocket expenses the next day but wondered if she could do without the steam iron that month which she was trying to purchase so that both of them could be well dressed like other living in the high rise neighborhood.

Munna, 40 Years, Auto Rickshaw Driver

Sonu's neighbor, Munna was unusually irritated that day. The fruit vendor from whom he was trying to purchase the water melon for his family was not ready to budge on the price by even a rupee. Munna knew that it was because of this location, which was considered to be one of the most upbeat ones in Gurugram, Haryana. The vendor was charging INR 100 for a piece of watermelon that would be available at INR 40 in the mandi from where he normally purchased his fruits and vegetables. He also knew that the outer cover of the water melon was polished and the one at the mandi was better: organic and fresh. He normally would never purchase fruits that were not seasonal as he had grown up with the belief that the best fruits in terms of quality and price were seasonal fruits. He was also aware that these would be easy to digest. He took care not to buy too early at the start of a season as many fruits were artificially ripened by injecting chemicals. He also did not purchase toward the end of the season as the decaying process started. Munna lived along with Sonu and others in the Moti Vihar of Silokhera village. It was a large slum in Sector 30, Gurugram. He belonged to a family of four members comprising of two children; a girl named Radha of eight years and a boy named Vijay of four years. Radha and Vijay went to a nearby private school. Munna and his wife Rani realized that to improve the quality of life, studies and education were vital. Shopping for the household was a monthly recreational event where the family went together and purchased the majority of the consumables for the household. The consumables largely comprised of grocery, fruits, and vegetables. If any item fell short in between Munna would purchase it through a kirana store. It was more because of convenience related reasons rather than any other that he purchased through a kirana store. Earlier he used to travel to Sadar Bazaar, the main old marketplace of Gurugram. Gurugram till the year 2000 was semi-rural town in Haryana adjoining Delhi with a population of 1.5 million. Rapid growth through the IT enabled call centers set up by various multinational corporations saw massive urban infrastructure development. The city got an inflow of both jobs and money. Commercial and residential structures bloomed but the city catered to all kind of inhabitants; locals and immigrants, rich and poor, white collar and blue collar, young and old. Munna was a local and had been driving auto rickshaw since the year 1999. The city limits and the population were scanty then and so was the business. With the advancement in city's profile he got more business per day over the last 20 years yet his cost of living also increased severely and now he also faced the threat from other auto rickshaw drivers whose numbers had increased substantially. The auto rickshaw drivers were basically from the states of Uttar Pradesh, Bihar, Jharkhand, and West Bengal where there was little development and employment opportunities were also low. Munna enjoyed special shopping occasions in contrast to the routine ones. Special occasions comprised shopping for festivals, and so on, and for items such as clothes and accessories including electronic items. Apart from convenience at the local kirana the major reason for Munna to make the shift to neighborhood kirana store from Sadar Bazaar was the similarity of the prices at both the places. Earlier there was a difference: Sadar stores offered products at a substantial lower price whether local or branded as compared to the other stores. It was only when there was a need to purchase in bulk that he now decided to visit Sadar which was otherwise frequented on every Sunday some 10 years ago. Shopping for clothes, mobiles, and so on, were a purchase which the family enjoyed being together with. Considering each other's choices and bargaining with shopkeepers was no less fun than enjoying a Bollywood Hindi movie sitting in the front row. It was the shared experience between the family and the marketplace but came only once or twice a year during major Hindu festivals such as Diwali in autumn and Holi in the spring season. The family at times even traveled to Karol Bagh, New Delhi which was almost 40 kilometers from Gurugram to get better variety, quality, and cheaper price. Rani was very particular about saving money and little did she mind the time, money, and effort that it took to travel through the overcrowded bus or metro through the entire Sunday, which was the only day that the family had as a common holiday which could be spent together. They felt satisfied when they purchased in such a manner and got okay products at okay rates within their budget, of a desired quality, suited to the occasion for which it was purchased. Contented with their life and purchases such as this Munna and Rani often wondered if their entire life time would just be in arranging the needs of the family; education, marriage, food, health, and so on. Did they even matter as a big section of the society to members of other sections? Was there any system for giving social security for them? Who was responsible for them or were they just left to fend for them to survive?

Rani, 38 Years, Cook

Munna's wife Rani was a supportive spouse, a providing mother, and a sincere lady. She worked in the high rise apartments around her colony as a cook and had by now become an expert in multi state cuisine as her customers belonged to a cosmopolitan group. Over a decade and half of her work experience she had learned to cook Gujrati, Marathi, South Indian (Kerala, Tamil Nadu, Telangana, and Andhra Pradesh) and North Indian (Punjab, Haryana, Bihar, Uttar Pradesh, and Madhya Pradesh) recipes. Originally a Bengali, she could only visit her native town in West Bengal, once in every two years when she had saved a considerable amount of INR 50,000 or more that would help the family to travel and pump that money into the pucca house being built there that was her father's dream. Living in one room accommodation in Silokhera village in Gurugram, Rani had vowed that she will not let Radha and Vijay lead the same kind of life as hers and would work hard along with her husband to get them proper education and lifestyle. She often took her children to the households where she worked in Sujjan Vihar so that they are exposed to an upscale environment and be inspired to achieve that. Rani told her employer that her only motivation to work from morning 8:00 a.m. to evening 8:00 p.m. was to give a good life to her children; a life full of security, peace, and respect, a life where children do not feel helpless for nobody to provide or stand up for and could stand up for themselves; confident and bright. Rani made it a point to give her children the best and she was as hard pressed for time or even more than Neetu, the lady for whom she cooked for in Sujjan Vihar. Neetu was a corporate lawyer juggling between schedules. Rani had taken the full responsibility of the kitchen including the health and nutrition of the family and often decided what should be prepared for lunch and dinner that would also suit the taste along with health and nutrition of the daughter Smriti 11 years, husband Rajeev 45 years and mother-in-law Raka aged 85 years. Neetu's family lived in Sujjan Vihar on rent in a three bedroom flat in one of the most costliest sector of Gurugram, Sector 43. The rent was INR 37,500 per month in 2018. The family's annual income was around INR 4,800,000. Rani was employed at an income of INR 4,500 per month for cooking twice a day with two holidays in a month. Rani often took more than two holidays, around 3–4 but that was okay with Neetu who understood it was difficult to take care of family and individual needs in just two holidays. Working in a combination of once and twice a day in several households Rani could earn around INR 15,000 per month same as her husband Munna. The per capita income for the family was around $4 per day. Neetu always purchased ITC Aashirwad whole wheat atta priced at INR 320 per kilogram. Rani normally purchased loose atta from Sadar Bazaar or would some time purchase wheat, clean it, and get it grounded at the local neighborhood flour mill. The price of this atta would be around INR 20 per kilogram, quality was absolutely pure since from procurement of wheat till the grinding entire process happened in front of her through her involvement. The process took almost 40 hours. With heavy duty hours time was now a constraint for Rani, so she had started purchasing loose flour from the local kirana store in her vicinity at a slightly higher price than INR 20 per kilogram. This was a very convenient option but lately Munna had started complaining of a stomach ache and twice in the present month he fell sick after consuming rotis made from that flour. Though not for sure but Rani somehow doubted the quality of the atta from the local kirana store. She occasionally used to purchase the two kilograms ITC Aashirwaad atta pack the same brand as Neetu from the same Sujjan Vihar shop. She would do this when there would be a shortfall before the close of the month or when she had some extra money. It satisfied her extremely as she mentioned to Neetu that they also consume the same brand as hers. Using this product gave her a sense of pride, dignity, and self-respect but now she thought that it would become necessary to switch as her husband's health was concerned.

There were a few times in a month (2–3) when the family visited Sadar or the local mandi to purchase the monthly grocery in bulk. Occasional short falls were met from the kirana store.

Taal, 15 Years, Domestic Help

Rani's sentiment was echoed by Taal the 16-year-old girl who worked as an eight-hour domestic help in Neetu's household. Living in Gurugram's Kanhai village near Sector 43 she everyday saw girls of her age going to college wearing dresses of latest fashion trends. She particularly liked the ankle length trousers, tapering on the ankle and snuggling on the slim waist just below the belly button combined with a hanging broad shouldered top. The best color combination she thought was the black trouser with the white top in contrast to her friend who considered red better with black. This was one of the usual topics of their conversation in the 20 minutes walk from her one room shanty which was inhabited by five people to Neetu's colony in Sector 43, Gurugram, one of the most affluent locations. Taal's family consisted of her parents and sisters one younger and elder by two years each. Apart from these five inhabitants of her family in Gurugram she had three more siblings. The eldest sister was married and lived in a separate room with her husband and daughter in the same location ata slight distance from Taal's house. The two younger ones lived in West Bengal with their grandmother and went to a local school there. The boy was aged eight years and the girl was nine years. Taal's mother Nachamma worked as a domestic help but not for long hour in a single household. She did the cleaning which is normally done manually in countries such as India in contrast to the developed countries where it is done through vacuum cleaners. Given the Indian climate that had conditions of dust and moisture prevalent especially in the North; cleaning that included brooming, dusting, and mopping was an everyday activity in the households. The changes in the socioeconomic structure of social classes now saw an increase in the number of professional working women such as Neetu in Gurugram. The routine household chores such as cooking and cleaning of the house which were traditionally done by the lady of the house in most of the Indian social classes were now outsourced thus creating employment and livelihood opportunities for people like

Taal, Nachamma, and Rani. They worked full time, that is, 8–12 hours a day or part time 3–4 hours a day. While Taal worked for eight hours in Neetu's house, Nachamma worked for 3–4 hours doing the cleaning across five houses in the same apartments. Rest of the time was used for looking after the family. Taal's father was a cycle-rickshaw puller and Nachamma and he together could manage an income of INR 10,000 per month. The youngest sister was just five years old who whiled away her time all through the day playing with other children in the neighborhood or her parents and sisters, when they were available. The average per person per capita income was close to $2 per day. Taal had gone to school till class five when they were in West Bengal but the extreme impoverished conditions had forced the family to look for resettlement and search of better employment opportunities had brought them to Gurugram where some of her father's friends were already working. It was true that they made a better living here and was proud of the fact that she was the maximum earner for the household at INR 8,500 per month. Her lady was also very cordial and respectful to her unlike the previous one who treated her like a door mat. Taal was very upset with the ex-boss and was happy that within two months of her coming to Gurugram she had got such a nice job. Neetu had three conditions for Taal: one the ability to talk in Hindi as her 85-year-old mother-in-law could follow no other language, punctuality, and hygiene of the girl. Taal understood these well and adhered to them with particular emphasis. She had patiently learnt all the other ways of the household and with great responsibility took care of the needs of each and every member of the family. Yet it was difficult for her to absorb all the glamour that the city offered, dress was only one facet. The present lifestyle seemed so comfortable that though it had once pained to leave the school and the company of her friends but the luxury of air conditioned rooms and watching television throughout the day had helped her quickly forget the pain. She wondered when her household could afford an air conditioner as bearing the evening heat from May till September after the day spent in air conditioner was not comfortable at all. She often shared with her mother the experience of sitting in the car which she got when she accompanied the family in their outings. Nachamma told her that she should also own one in future but wondered how could that be possible; through a lottery ticket, a rich husband, or luck as without education it was sure that Taal would not get any other employment-related growth opportunities with only marginal inflationary increase in incomes.

Ranjana, 46 Years, Cook and Geeta, 38 Years, Housekeeping Staff

The view of Taal was echoed by Ranjana, a cook like Rani who also worked a part timer in Sujjan Vihar. Ranjana and her husband Shyam Palikar lived in Kanhai for the last 13 years. Ranjana had started working as a domestic help doing cleaning and dusting in households but had now graduated as a cook. Her husband worked as a housekeeping staff with a private concern in Gurugram. Both of them together could average around INR 25,000 per month. Ranjana's only dream was to earn a lot of money so that the family can have a comfortable and luxurious living like the families for whom she worked. She was sure that her daughter would be given the best education given her budget which she was working extra hard to increase by taking more number of households than an average cook would take. Her main problem happened because of her husband Shyam. Shyam was a decent man and cared for the family, but every night after getting heavily drunk he lost his senses, fought and argued with Ranjana who wanted him to stop drinking. Many of the days he would get violent and also beat Ranjana black and blue if she argued. He not only exhausted his money but also snatched her's often. Initially Ranajana would tolerate all this and at times helplessly cry and take it as her fate but after the birth of their daughter, Ranjana was a different lady. She equally fought with Shyam when he tried to snatch her money, sometimes she also would get him out of the house. He would normally return after a day or two. While these were the routine state of affairs Ranjana was now concerned also about the upbringing of her daughter who had turned two years recently. Now that she would turn sensible she did not want her to grow in such an environment where there was no peace and everyday fights were the routine. She wondered how could her daughter respect such parents and whether just sending her to school will help her becoming a strong and peaceful individual if it was not supported by a conducive environment at home. Often Ranjana shared her sentiment with her best friend and neighbor Geeta Ramasrey. Geeta and Ranjana shared a very close friendship of more than 13 years. Geeta belonged to Bahraich in Western Uttar Pradesh, the most widely populated state in northern

India. Although the family was traditionally involved in agriculture lately men and women of her and her husband's age had started moving to cities for employment. There was not sufficient income from the farms to feed a family of seven people: Geeta, her husband Ramasreay, her parents-in-law and three children. The two girls and one son were all under ten years of age. Geeta and her husband Ramasrey worked in farms with Geeta managing the household chores as well. They faced several problems with their farms such as the uncertainty of environment conditions, the bullying behavior of the middle men, falling rates of their produce, and shortage of land labor at peak times. All this had made the 42-year-old Ramasrey and 35-year-old Geeta to move to Gurugram like many others from their town. The couple moved with their children and the parents remained in the village as it was difficult for them to consider resettlement. They agreed to take care of the ancestral house and the farm with whatever resources possible as the income and the produce would suffice for the family. Even Geeta would bring quintals of wheat, rice and gallons of mustard oil for the entire year in two/three visits to the hometown. They would otherwise cost her almost three to four times with a different level of quality also that was not as pure as the one she got from her town. Geeta knew how important it was to earn money so that the condition of her children could improve. Geeta was totally illiterate whereas Ramasrey was educated till class fifth. The everyday struggles comprising of the fight for dignity, independence, satiating hunger and helpless poverty made her realize that growth and self-respect would only come from education and her children must get proper education. Ramasrey also seconded her sentiment as he had seen how Geeta was dependent for every small decision on him. Just to illustrate Geeta owned a feature phone version of a mobile handset from the Carbon company but she could only receive calls or dial two numbers that were coded 1 and 2, which was Ramasrey as an emergency contact and her father-in-law again for the same purpose. Normally people hold mobile handsets so that they are independent and connected irrespective of their surroundings. Here she was still dependent on her husband right from purchase till use, operation, and maintenance because lack of education and social upbringing had imbibed in her a severe inferiority complex. It is true that in traditional Indian households tasks have been divided in a manner that outdoor activities that need negotiations with members outside the family were done by the male who served as the master of the house. He was supported in his role by his wife who would take care of all members of the family including the relatives and neighbors and run the household chores in a given set of resources which would vary as per the socioeconomic structure of the segment. Geeta had worked in the village farms with her husband and father-in-law and now was working in the housekeeping department of an agency that took contractual housekeeping assignments from several corporate houses in Gurugram. She got a monthly salary of INR 5,000 per month with one weekly off on Sunday. If she took any other leave her wages would be deducted through a daily wage rate. Ramasrey worked as a labor/daily wager in a soap manufacturing company in Gurugram and earned around INR 10,000 per month. The per capita income was 1.33$ per person per day. Despite working an equal number of hours outside the house, Geeta still did the cooking and cleaning and took care of children. She would sometimes miss office because of physical fatigue but would also lose a share of her salary. Ramasrey was a supportive husband and tried to help Geeta in her household tasks but they were mainly Geeta's responsibility. Geeta continued in her secondary role comfortably, dependent on Ramasrey for a simple task such as operating a mobile phone leave alone purchasing one. Her only dream was to see her children well educated and settled with a better life than theirs. Her daughter would often fight with the two brothers for equal play which Geeta simply observed at times reprimanding her. Geeta would tell her to settle for less than her brothers and learn household chores while not telling the boys the same thing. Yet, silently deep inside her heart Geeta did not want her daughter to obey and was deeply satisfied on seeing her fight for fair and equal play.

Arjun, 17 Years, Housekeeping Staff

Geeta's brother Arjun often visited her sister's place. Although neither Geeta nor Arjun were allowed leaves apart from the weekly off on days designated by the contractor if there was no work in the client premises. Arjun and Geeta made a point to meet regularly at least once in a fortnight. Arjun was younger than Geeta and had just completed his 18th birthday. He worked in the housekeeping department of a private agency in Gurugram. He was not involved in the cooking and cleaning services but used to serve tea and meals in the organization's mess. If there was a party on the day of his weekly off his leave was canceled and there was no complimentary off for it. In such instances Geeta and Ramasrey would visit him with their children. Arjun got monthly salary of INR 7,000 per month and was provided accommodation by the contractor with meals in the client premises. There was one room in which five people would collect to retire in the night as their duty hours started from 8:00 a.m. in the morning and extended till 10:30 p.m. in the night with some light hours between the two meals, although they had sufficient kitchen related chores to be completed at that time. Arjun had studied till class eight in his village and had dropped schools for two reasons, one, he did not enjoy studies much, and two his parents could not afford his education. His father worked as a daily wage laborer and mother was a housewife. With growing years both his parents developed health problems resulting in the loss of livelihood. Arjun had come with his cousin Suraj who also worked with the same contractor in Gurugram, as there were no jobs in his native place which he could do. He was 15 years old then, he also hoped that he could live with his sister Geeta but that could not happen as space was already a constraint in her sister's household with three children, two adults and kitchen plus other household items crammed in one room which was charged INR 3,000 per month. The brother and sister understood each other's condition well and never shared any of their problems with their parents who thought their children were doing very well in the big city and often boasted about their status amongst the village folk. Over the years Arjun's mother's health also deteriorated and she could no longer do the household chores and had been pressing Arjun to marry so that Arjun's wife could take charge of her responsibilities and she could rest in peace. Being underage Arjun had been avoiding it but since last year the pressure was building up intensely as the mother's condition was worsening. Arjun agreed reluctantly yet he was not sure how would he handle things after marriage especially the finances. His family asked him not to worry as feeding one more person in the same ration would not create much disturbance in the present working arrangement. Arjun used to send INR 6,000 to his parents keeping INR 1,000 for his pocket expenses. The bride would take care of his parents and the household chores. Arjun would meet her once or twice a year when he visited his home town for a week/ten days. No one in the family ever considered the feelings and dreams of the newlywed girl who was coming only as a resource for the family. This settlement relieved Arjun of his financial anxieties but he could not understand why did he feel so excited and curious at the thought of getting married to a stranger and starting a new phase of his life, who would then become his companion for life. The initial years of marriage where couples bond in arranged marriages as in India were going to be consumed in the mechanics of arranging and providing for the family and he wondered whether marriage only meant a new set of worries after a few years like for his sister Geeta who toiled both in the house and at work so that the children were well educated and the family got a decent life. He for once wondered if he could bring his wife Durga to Gurugram along with his parents who could not live alone in the village so that both of them could work and stay together. But as he was reminded of his salary he dropped the idea because in INR 7,000 he could not fend for the family and accommodation both. It would only be possible after a few years by when Durga would have settled that they could consider this. It was important for them to first understand and know each other before taking any other step. He thought of patiently waiting till that time keeping his fingers crossed and hoping that Durga would understand his situation and decision.

Thinking of Arjun's marriage, Geeta was very excited. Arjun was her only brother and that too a pampered one because he was 20 years younger to her and she and her parents would not only accept his tantrums but also cover up for his pranks in the village as a child. The bonding between the four members of the family was very strong and tight. It is only because of circumstances and her marriage that they had physically been distanced but their hearts still resonated closely. Geeta's thoughts and excitements suddenly vanished with her youngest son shaking her and asking for a glass of water. She immediately came into reality. After giving her son water she sat on the "modha" (bamboo stick hand-crafted chair) slightly with a new stream of thoughts that caused worry and anxiety. Arjun's marriage would mean a big family event for which she and Ramasrey had not made any budget provision. The couple could earn only to make hands to mouth including the children's education. Arjun's marriage would mean a minimum expense of INR 50,000 with at least 15 days leave that should account for a loss of their monthly income. Being the elder married sister she would have to search for a decent wedding gift; ideally a jewelry piece such as gold necklace and two matching gold earrings or bangles. The cost of 10 grams of 24k gold (99.9 percent) in Delhi was around INR 32,250 in December 2018, more than the couple's income put together. Gold was not even thinkable as the jewelry set would cost in lakhs of rupees. Having ruled gold out she still had to think of a substitute gift item. She quickly recollected her parent's house in the village to be reminded of the minimum household gadgets. She knew that her parents had managed to get a second hand refrigerator, television, and cooler. In fact Geeta herself had purchased these items from the second hand sale for them. Washing machine was one item that her mother wanted to purchase as her neighbor had recently purchased and she saw the comfort of washing and drying clothes in extreme cold conditions. Geeta knew that her brother was not taking any dowry much against her parent's wishes. In fact this was the only condition on which Arjun had agreed for marriage against the normal prevalent practice where the bridegroom's family would ask both for cash and kind for their son as a customary dowry as in the village. People would ask exorbitant amounts and the tradition had slowly become a social menace for the parents of a girl child in North India. Geeta thought that she could gift a second hand washing machine that would come in the price range of INR 7,000-10,000 as a fully automatic version. Parallelly she was also thinking if there could be any excuse possible that could be made and her family could skip the marriage altogether, although she would deeply miss it. The other expenses would involve journey tickets from one destination to other including the local conveyance. Although the ticket rates for bus from the district railway station to her town were lower than the air conditioned deluxe bus rates from Gurugram bus depot to Anand Vihar railway terminal in New Delhi, yet a total expense of INR 4,000–5,000 would be incurred in the total end-to-end travel. She would also have to purchase clothes worth the occasion; that would include more than one as local marriages in the villages were still done in the traditional manner. That would mean at least three set of dresses for her children and one for Ramasrey and her. They could manage with the older dresses that she had kept since her marriage which happened 15 years back. The fashion and styles had changed but the heavy Benarsi sari was still glamorous. She remembered how beautiful she looked as a bride then. One new sari she would definitely need for the main function, other side events she could manage with the older things. She planned a similar pattern for Ramasrey and was satisfied that she had not sold her gold jewelry last year to arrange for the land property for her in-laws who were keen on it. She was thankful to her husband Ramasrey who had not forced her for it. The total expenses for clothes for the family would come to around INR 15,000. How happy and satisfied she felt at the thought of her children wearing new clothes with tidy hair and matching footwear. She took extra care that her children were always groomed well whether it be school, play, or party. Her village folks would get jealous on seeing such bright and beautiful kids. Such moments were of extreme pride and achievement for her as it felt that she had achieved a feat which was not easy, though she also knew that it was not only appearance but also physical hygiene of the children which they had to be aware of and keep well as a matter of habit for successful life.

Savita and Motiram; 36 and 40 Years, Part Time Domestic Help and Housekeeping Staff

Geeta thought of calling Savita her neighbor with whom she often went to Sadar for shopping. Sadar was the flea market of Gurugram and the only typical "bazaar," the market place which Indian households were used to for shopping. Before Gurugram became the millennial city it was like any other small town of India and people visited Sadar for all kind of purchases in a total contrast to a mall. Right from the AC environment of closed doors with brands Sadar was an open market with numerous shops and "feriwallahs"—street vendors as a beehive which could only be mastered by bees. Humid, clumsy, and irritating could be the words to best describe the environment yet Geeta and Savita's children enjoyed the day there as it was the break from the routine and they could also enjoy some roadside chai and jalebi though there were a lot of houseflies over them. They also knew that if mummy was taking them for shopping it would mean that they would be entitled to some clothes and other goodies as well. Savita normally visited Sadar once a month regularly for purchasing monthly grocery for the household. Normally this was done around a Sunday close to 7th of every month because her husband got his salary on the 7th. The shortfall of any grocery item would be fulfilled through the neighborhood kirana store. It not only offered convenience of saving distance and travel time but also the item could be purchased on credit which was not possible at the Sadar store. Based on long years of familiarity the kirana owner knew that Savita would definitely pay back in the next month, and would not create any fuss on giving items on credit. Little did the shop owner realize that Savita very well understood that he charged at least 10 percent more on that product. Thinking her to be illiterate and ignorant he made her sign on the increased MRP and would also charge an interest if the credit was not returned within a month. Illiterate she was but she was not a fool and would clearly understand the foul play of the shopkeeper yet continued and in times of need she had to resort to this help quite often. Savita and her husband Motiram ran their household in clearly defined roles. Grocery purchase which was done in bulk was his husband's responsibility both because it was bulk purchase and involved discretion to spend money and do the purchase wisely. Such decisions which involved more wisdom went into the male bastion in such households. It was assumed that women either have lesser developed intellect or cannot use it properly. Clothes for herself and her children were purchased by Savita in a budgeted amount. Normally the price was the most important factor beyond fitting, fabric, and style. If the dress was slightly loose or tight Savita would alter it herself. If the fabric was slightly uncomfortable she would reprimand her children for being overtly demanding and they should learn to adjust. Normally the purchase was done from the kiosks/stalls put up outside the shops where shopkeepers use to put pieces up at discounted prices. There would be minor defects or problems in the pieces but they would not be easily noticeable. Normally there was no store loyalty that Savita had developed or any store preference but yes the behavior of the salesperson was important to her.

Sadar was a place where even well-to-do families visited for availability of wide variety of items at very low prices. Even ladies of houses which had an annual income of INR 50,000 per month and above would come. Savita disliked the way these people behaved with people of her income class. They would always push her and children, speak in a humiliating manner, and at times even swear at them if their voices were not heard. Savita was very irritated especially when she and a shopkeeper were negotiating a purchase and such a customer would come to the shop. The shopkeeper would immediately stop attending her and start attending the new customer. It felt so humiliating as if she had no respect or worth. She did not mind waiting for her turn if it was fair but this behavior she found unfair. Her children would sometimes notice the tears and even fight with the shopkeeper but Savita would just leave the place. She was very clear that nothing was more important in life than dignity and self-respect and she wanted her children to learn the same values. Motiram was not very pleased at such behavior. He sometimes chided sometimes slowly explained to Savita that she should not be so arrogant as ladies need to be submissive and why should she fight even if somebody behaved roughly with her. She needed to use more wisdom by seeing the value in purchase rather in shopkeeper behavior. Savita would patiently listen trying to reason out if she really did any wrong and though she did not say so but she did not believe that she was wrong. Savita knew and would always try to understand Motiram. She realized how difficult it was for him to accept that he alone could not provide for the family despite trying hard he could only manage INR 10,000 per month by working as a cleaner (cleaning cars) in the high rise apartments of Gurugram along with doubling up as a gardener in the same society. He knew that Savita who earned INR 5,000 per month by doing the cleaning of five households could also earn INR 5,000 more if she did not have to manage the household. Though Motiram was a reasonable man and understood that women can be equal yet it was difficult at times for him to let his wife be an equal. Their households had all the necessary items in the single room be it the refrigerator or television although all had been arranged from the second hand market. The room was available at INR 3,000 per month but they had to separately pay for the electricity bill. Vegetables were purchased from the local weekly haat. Haat is a place on the street where vendors would retail vegetables either procured from the mandi, some intermediary wholesaler, or direct farmer. Normally the prices were cheaper compared to the bigger stores and many times after 9 p.m. they would get vegetables at one third the market rate. Motiram and Savita many times visited the "haat" at that particular time. Savita enjoyed shopping so much and was a fun loving person. Although the situations and conditions in her life had made her quite sober yet her basic fun-filled nature often overtook her. She was happy when her children showed excitement and fun in shopping. Visiting Sadar, she herself would become a child trying to purchase each and every item on her wish list, exceeding her budget and counseling herself on buying another item next time of slightly lower amount. She would explain this to Motiram as she knew that he would otherwise scold her. She was an efficient householder best managing her household need and resources. Her most satisfying moment would be when she could find an item that was missing for her family like the bean bag which her son had been searching since the time he had sat in one of her master's house. Although there was no room for it either in her home or budget and she had no courage to ask Motiram for it. She felt that her prayer had been answered when one day one of her masters gave a used bean bag to her. They were going to dispose it when Savita mentioned that she would take it.

Charanjeet Singh, 41 Years, Security Guard and Jayanti, Security Guard

Motiram often used to discuss his condition and psyche with Charanjeet Singh; the security guard from Ballia, U.P. Charanjeet was a more open man in terms of his understanding on life and outlook toward society and gender roles. He believed men and women have been made equals as human beings and should enjoy space, rights, and respect in society. He treated his wife with great respect and equality and she also contributed equally in terms of caring and earning for the family. Charanjeet often chided Motiram for his chauvinistic ways. Motiram understood that when he got irrational, Charanjeet could pull him to reason. Charanjeet had been working as a security guard with a private security agency in Gurugram and lived in Kanhai in a one room accommodation with his wife and two children, one aged 17 years and another 12 years, both boys. He earned a monthly salary of INR 11,000 per month and his wife earned INR 12,000 per month. She also worked as a security guard in a private hospital. Both of them were employed with the same security agency but were placed with different clients. Charanjeet did not mind his wife doing the same job as him and a slightly increased salary. In fact both of them had left Ballia in 2007 in hope of improving their family life especially the growth and development of their kids. Both of them had decided that they would send money every month for Charanjeet's parents who could manage themselves well in the village with the parental house and some farms. Charanjeet's father was healthy enough to look after them. They had decided to share their roles and duties in terms of both opting for work so that their income increases. The family today could manage a per capita income of $1.6 per day. They would also share the household roles. The couple would jointly do the cooking after returning from work after 9:00 p.m. They tried to keep their work shifts from 8:00 a.m. to 8:00 p.m. they would cook the vegetable/side dish for the morning and while Jayanti his wife would do the remaining cooking, Charanjeet would start doing the cleaning and assisting the kids in getting ready for school. Charanjeet and Jayanti had made many changes in their dietary habits. They had stopped consuming "arhardaal," a special pulses category that was consumed daily as a part of their village cuisine. They had stopped eating it for two reasons; one the assurance in the city on the variety available was not there the way it was in their village. Second it was too costly, at a rate on INR 120 per kilogram they could not afford it. In the village it was available at INR 30 per kilogram. The cost of living in the extravagant satellite metro town had forced people like Charanjeet to switch to local alternatives. Given the paucity of time Charanjeet now purchased the routine items from local neighborhood kirana stores. He would not do it from the smaller stores but the bigger stores (in terms of size) as he thought that he got both quality and variety. He also knew that he could purchase bigger SKU sizes of the monthly household grocery at bulk discounts which would normally not be available at the smaller stores. The smaller stores also raised the prices for offering convenience to the customer. This sense of getting more at a lesser price also made him more store loyal and the familiarity slowly started converting into relationships, although the root of this relationship as Charanjeet clearly knew was price. The retailer was assured of repeat business and though he offered bulk discounts he still made profits more than the Sadar Bazaar retailer as the prices were slightly high and in absence of going to Sadar people like Charanjeet started purchasing from these stores. Sometimes the retailer used to adjust prices and offered on credit and sometimes Charanjeet would adjust for a product or brand that was unavailable and either wait or settle for the next best alternative. But apart from the grocery and vegetables for any other kind of purchase the couple went to Sadar. He was also very clear in letting the decision related to clothes purchased be taken by Pushpa, his wife, as experience had taught that certain decisions are "ladies" decisions not because of any other reasons but preferences. Grocery was a "male" decision. For clothes he only went to either the shops that he already knew or Sadar as they would offer him the best value in the cheapest price. Grocery was a male decision also because it involved interactions with the shopkeeper. Even clothes purchase would involve that but that was once a while whereas the former was more regular in nature. Charanjeet used to purchase earlier from a "Bihari" kiranawalla but realized that he was being exploited. The store owner used to give items on credit but charged three times more. Charanjeet now switched to another store although he knew he was being treated unfair even here in terms of service and prices yet the degree of exploitation (being charged roughly 10 percent more on credit) was lesser and tolerable. Charanjeet knew that this was the standard operating style and the benchmark was them was this level. Charanjeet used to stay in a one room accommodation like many others in Kanhai village, Gurugram. There was a total of 300 plus rooms in the five acre land. Apart from paying a rent of INR 3,000–4,000, the tenants had to purchase vegetables from the landlord's vegetable shop. Though there were cheaper options for vegetables available in the locality but the unsaid rule was that all tenants had to purchase from this shop or else the room was not available. Though Charanjeet felt exploited and frustrated yet he had no choice because it was the same situation at other locations as well. He knew the only way out of this was to have a proper education that should lead to a decent job and salary. Respect and power to stand for one's rights would automatically come. Whenever possible he should do the change and both he and his wife were working only toward providing the best education and lifestyle for their boys. Charanjeet also as a good practice tried to avoid items on credit though it was not always possible. A person of strong values he believed to live within one's limited resources keeping aspirations within control. As a necessary requirement of contemporary times, Charanjeet did keep a smartphone but a low budget one and did not even aspire for a high budget one like others. Charanjeet challenged stereotypes. Hailing from a Rajput lineage Charanjeet did not mind Pushpa working and always gave her the desired respect, treated as an equal in all household decisions, and even defended her as and when required in a patriarchal set up. He equally contributed in household chores and never complained of certain tasks to be done by males or females as other family members. The entire neighborhood comprised of people of similar profiles including many of his own relatives who had followed him the pursuit of leading a good life. Some of them worked in more than one occupations also to maximize their earnings in hope of a better lifestyle. Ultimately they all worked very hard to get their children educated as they believed education would ultimately lead to happiness. Many of them including Charanjeet knew how they got exploited at various places including their jobs because they could not fight as they had limited alternatives for jobs otherwise. The security agency in which Charanjeet worked took its share in two parts, one legal; the fixed component plus the commission from the client and second from the employee's salary which was almost 10–15 percent of his salary on an average. Job in the security agency was tough as both Charanjeet and his wife worked in a twelve hour shift with no holidays. He went to his hometown once in two years and took a break of one–two months with no salary for the couple. He believed in continuing with the same job despite facing such extremes as he knew the ways of business and believed that staying in the same place brought credibility to the person along with position, authority, and responsibility. He was content with his life and prayed to God to continue showering his blessings and maintain his life full of honesty and respect. Charanjeet during his purchases did consider the manner in which the shopkeeper treated him.

Nihaal, 18 Years, Housekeeping Staff

While Charanjeet and Pushpa wanted their sons to study, Nihaal the elder one, 17 years of age somehow was not interested in studies at all. The younger one aged 12 years was studying well in class seven. Much against the wishes of his parents Nihaal joined a private housekeeping firm in Gurugram. He was more attached to his mother than father. He told Pushpa that it was difficult for him to continue education right after class eighth. It was difficult for him to follow what the teacher explained in class and there was no help at home. Both the parents went to work early and returned late at night. When Pushpa had noticed Nihaal losing interest in studies, she had tried to arrange for tuition classes but several factors let it not happen. Apart from finances it was difficult for Pushpa to motivate Nihaal for it. Though Nihaal understood that his future life and its growth prospects were dependent on his educational qualification yet he could not fight the distractions given by his friends who spent the entire day on mobiles and roaming here and there. Few of them also came from well-to-do families so money was not a constraint. Nihaal thought he could help his mother slightly by taking a job which would also ease his sense of guilt. Nihaal sometimes assisted his mother as a coolie for her shopping chores. These were times when Charanjeet was not present and Nihaal would drive her mother to the mandi on his bicycle. Pushpa alone would do the purchase as it was difficult for Nihal to identify a yellow turdaal from a yellow moongdaal. He could only purchase items which his mother instructed him in detail. He was very particular about bargaining for price as otherwise people would deceive. He particularly did not like the fact when the shopkeeper behaved rudely because of him being "poor." The only shopping trips he enjoyed were for clothes and accessories. He would buy the latest trends, cheapest clothes available in the haat. Nihaal was very particular about purchasing food items. This was one category where he satisfied price for health. The condition and ambience of the market or store hardly mattered to him. What mattered the most was the best price deal across most of the products but he would never return to the shops where the shopkeeper had behaved badly with him earlier.

Now that the Urban Indian BOP customer and his lifestyle can be visualized it becomes important to find out what motivates or drives him toward purchase, satisfaction, and happiness. To achieve this a grounded theory study was designed which is being detailed in the section below.

Methodology

The study adopted grounded theory approach to understand the urban BOP consumers in the context of India. A qualitative approach is supposedly more appropriate in this kind of setting when the said phenomenon is at nascent stage (Ireland 2008). The consumers in this segment, must be studied in their own right (Hart and Sharma 2004). Many researchers too have propounded that a different research approach should be adopted to study such markets, for example, Sheth (2011), Gebauer and Reynoso (2013) and Fisk et al. (2016), and so on. Grounded theory approach was finally decided as it leads to the discovery of theory from data which is systematically obtained and analyzed in social research and wherein the theory produced is grounded in data (Glaser and Strauss 1967; Glaser 1978; Creswell 1998; Dey 1999).

To begin with grounded theory approach, a theoretical sample of 15 participants, was drawn from the Indian Urban BOP households with an average size of five members and with an annual income less than or equal to Indian Rupees 3,00,000.[1] The said sample size qualified the acceptable norm of 12–15 interviews (Glaser 1978). These participants were living in the city of Gurgaon[2] and were primarily employed in the unorganized sectors of India. These participants were primarily employed in unorganized sector in India. The said urban BOP represents 20 percent of the Indian BOP population The profile of these participants is as follows:

Semi-structured in-depth interviews were conducted with the said participants as mentioned in Table 2.1 in their native language that is, Hindi, as the participants were not well-versed in the English language. It was important to understand where, when, why, and how they normally made a purchase with reference to the purchase basket consisting of products across categories for example, grocery, perishables, and basic consumer durables, and so on. These product categories constituted 95 percent of their purchase basket.

The interviews revolved around following set of questions:

- How did they shop typically for different kinds of products?
- What were the major considerations in their purchase decision making?
- What was their purchase process like?
- What made them happy in their purchase?

---

[1]   Urban BOP as defined by Unitus Ventures, available at *https://unitus.vc/resources/defining-base-of-the-economic-pyramid-in-india/*

[2]   Gurgaon (officially Gurugram) is a satellite city of Delhi located in the Indian state of Haryana and is part of the National Capital Region (NCR) of India. It is characterized with cosmopolitan population, rapid urbanization, and with the third-highest per capita income in India. Of late, it has become the leading financial and industrial hub in India.

Table 2.1 Participants profile

Participant	Gender	Occupation	Literacy level	Language proficiency (Hindi)
1	Male	Autorickshaw driver	Basic	Speak, read, and write
2	Male	Security guard	Basic	Speak, read, and write
3	Female	Housekeeping Staff (Cleaning washrooms)	Illiterate	Speak
4	Female	Cook	Basic	Speak, read, and write
5	Female	Housekeeping staff (cleaning washrooms)	Illiterate	Speak
6	Male	Housekeeping staff (cleaning car)	Basic	Speak, read, and write
7	Male	Housekeeping staff (cleaning car)	Basic	Speak, read, and write
8	Male	Autorickshaw driver	Basic	Speak, read, and write
9	Male	Autorickshaw driver	Basic	Speak, read, and write
10	Female	Cook	Illiterate	Speak
11	Male	Autorickshaw driver	Basic	Speak, read, and write
12	Male	Housekeeping	Illiterate	Speak
13	Female	Non-working	Graduation	Speak, read, and write
14	Female	Domestic help	Illiterate	Speak
15	Female	Domestic help	Illiterate	Speak

- What gave them satisfaction? and so on.

Memos were written through the transcripts to generate labels and to draw interpretations. It was an iterative exercise wherein each transcript was subjected to constant comparison. Each transcript was first analyzed to prepare initial notes and identify the emergent open codes. Accordingly, the next participant was chosen. If need felt, changes incorporated in interviewing style and in probing whereas the broad questions

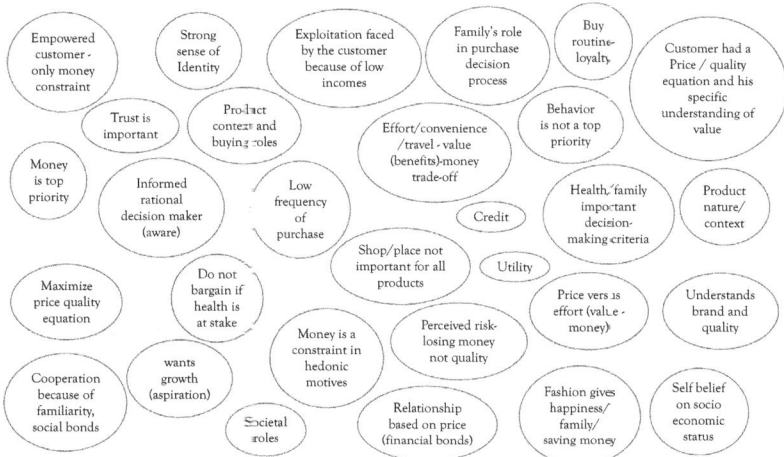

Figure 2.1 Open codes to understand the Indian urban BoP consumer behavior

remained the same as mentioned above. No software was used to translate the transcripts as the meaning could have got lost in the attempt and the entire study, thus was done manually. The analysis led authors to emergent themes from open codes through selective codes. These themes are presented, together with verbatim quotes from participants, to provide insights about pre- and post-purchase behavior of consumers at urban BOP.

Analysis and Discussion

As mentioned, each transcript was subjected to constant comparison wherein data were coded in every way possible. Line by line coding was followed, as recommended by Glaser (1978) and initial labels were attached to the data. The said line by line coding freed us from pre-conceptions and forced a real intimacy with the data. The emergent open codes could flush out what was important and point to directions in the analysis that may not have been thought of initially. Figure 2.1 depicts the open codes which were generated manually through interview transcripts.

The open codes were subsequently grouped in larger codes as the aim was to build a theory based on them. Glaserian version of grounded theory was followed that led to the selective coding stage after open coding.

Selective coding was done at a stage when there were no new open codes suggesting themselves and definite themes were emerging; categories become saturated at this stage. Glaser 1978 defines selective coding as the stage when coding is limited to only those categories that relate to the core category. Figure 2.2 depicts the selective codes which were generated from the open codes.

Based on the selective codes it was interpreted that the urban BOP Indian consumer was an aware and informed discretionary consumer, who could understand things well. S/He was a rational decision maker

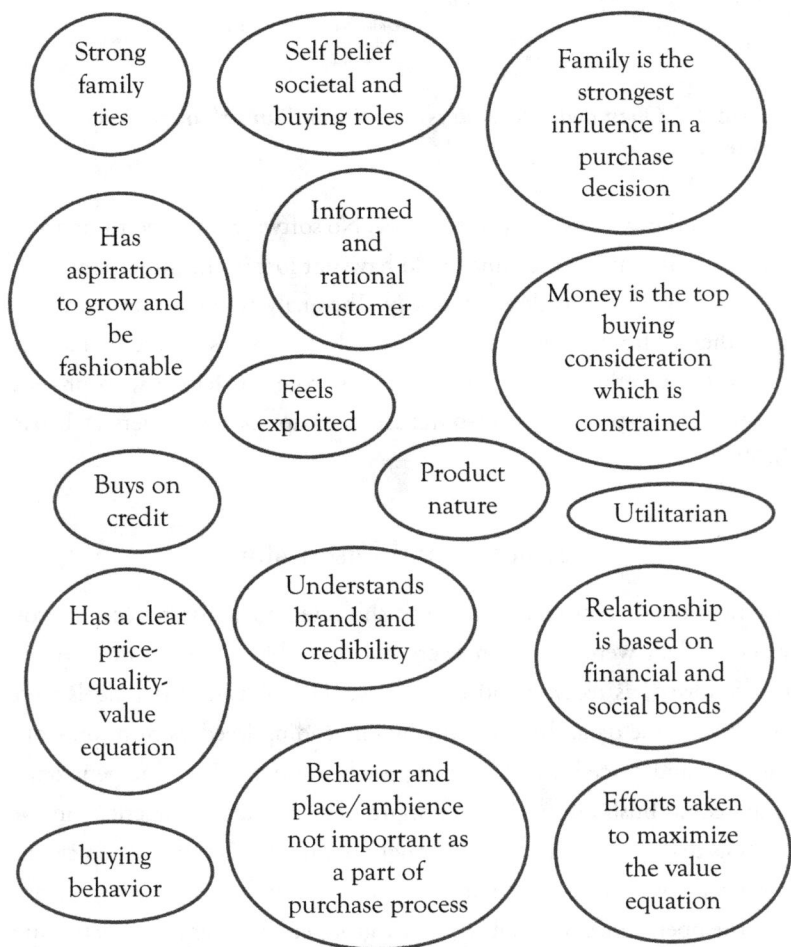

Figure 2.2 Selective codes to understand the Indian urban BoP consumer behavior

and her/his decision was basically hinged on money and family. Money was a resource and a constrained resource in this case. It is important to mention here that because of a line by line open coding procedure, there were multiple categories generated. Grouping of categories and initial abstraction of theory was started which led to theoretical coding. In the said iteration, we returned many times to open codes when we were grouping the themes (Charmaz 2006).

Theoretical coding is the stage when emergent substantive codes start relating to each other leading to theory generation, basis on the relationship(s) between the constructs and theoretical saturation is achieved. At this stage, six foundational premises (FPs) were evolved which has been explicated in the following section.

Foundational Premises (FPs) about the Indian Urban BOP Consumers

FP1: The urban BOP consumer in India is an informed discretionary consumer

This FP tells that the customer in this segment has information across the interviewed product categories to enable him to make a decision related to purchase even if it comes to latest news and products as can be observed through the following excerpt from one of the interviews,

> *Madam, what about us, we purchase from our neighborhood markets and stores as we have been doing for so many years. We get okay things at okay rates otherwise we sometimes also buy Patanjali[3] Flour as it is good quality, we are trying it.*

This customer understands quality and is also ready to pay extra if he is convinced or it else he will not buy. Since the customer lifestyle is

---

[3] Patanjali is the latest FMCG brand in India and is perceived as pure and traditional, drawn on the multidimensional brand equity of Indian Ayurveda, Sage Patanjali and Baba Ramdev, a well-known Yoga Guru. Patanjali Flour was available at INR 22 per kilogram compared to loose flour available at retail outlets for INR 16 per kilogram.

comparable to other consumable classes in the urban centers he is exposed to information and is not unaware though may have little formal education. He also exercises his discretion in taking a purchase decision.

FP2: Money is a constrained resource and top decision-making priority when it comes to making a purchase decision

Disposable income definitely is a constrained resource and gets maximum weightage while evaluating a purchase decision. This is reflected in the following interview excerpt;

> *We purchase loose rice, just check the quality there only by feel, smell and touch of rice. Grocery typically is purchased monthly by my husband from the (flea market) Sadar. If it is more that money in our hand, we drop some items or if they are costly and cross our budget, we again drop certain items. Satisfaction happens if we are able to purchase all our necessities in our budget. Happiness happens when our children wear new clothes, which we are able to purchase within our pocket, and look good. It is very satisfying to see that the children look decent, well covered and groomed. At least they are looking and living properly and we are able to provide for them, otherwise even that is a challenge. We are working toward them having a better life, they be educated and live well, not like us. It is so difficult to make a living in the cities, which are costly and villages which have no employment or facilities.*

FP3: Value for BOP customer only constitutes hard benefits (product related), equated to the price paid for the complete offering

The ambience, service, store, brand-related factors do not really influence their decisions. It is ultimately what they are getting for the price they are paying with reference to the household needs.

"*How does the shop or the shopkeeper matter, whoever gives me the maximum is where I purchase from*"

Above is his basic premise for making a purchase and he is willing to make an extra effort in terms of spending time and covering distance for such utility. Thus his satisfaction is basically utilitarian in nature as proposed in the FP 4.

FP4: The satisfaction is basically utilitarian in nature

FP5: Family is the key concern in any purchase-related decision making

In almost all the interviews with 15 participants across product categories such as daily household items including perishables and groceries, basic consumer durables and apparel the main driver that sets the expectation is around the concern for family. Simple statements such as the following from the transcripts highlight this,

> *Ultimately we want our children to be educated, happy and secure that is why we are ready to work extra even under exploitative conditions so that they can get education and shelter. Our landlord charges us not only rent for the house but also forces to buy vegetables and fruits from his own shop in the locality, which is selling them even at slightly higher prices than what we may be able to bargain and get at other shops in the neighborhood, but we have been living in his house for some years and he offers us credit and time even if we are not able to make timely payments, my child also goes to a nearby school. While we know he is acting unfair, we still would continue as otherwise we do not have the financial strength to relocate. Our children would not do this and that is why we are educating them.*

> *I buy grocery from the flea market as per the instruction of my mother, I dropped out of school and am working so that I can help my mother in making our ends meet. While buying grocery, I see that it should be okay by smelling and touching the grains such as rice, wheat and dals (pulses) but buy in bulk from the shop that gives me the best rates.*

FP6: There is an existent relationship between the retailer and the BOP urban customer

While this segment is not directly exposed to the manufacturer or main source of supply many times in the cities it has a relationship history with the unorganized trade/retailers serving them over number of years and credit terms. They continue to buy from them for reasons of familiarity and credit even at exploitative terms.

> *The shop or the shopkeeper is really immaterial but he is important because he gives me items in the end of the month even when I do not*

have money as my salary is exhausted. I buy from him for this reason, how he speaks does not matter even if he is rude or I do not like.

It emerged *that Concern for Family and Price are two anchor points* around which the purchase decision revolved and value for him was essentially benefits vs. costs (monetary). The interview excerpts are only highlighting the FP which is otherwise resultant of the selective codes.

Theoretical Integration: BOP Urban Indian Customer and Zone of Tolerance Model for His Expectations

The Urban Bottom of the Pyramid customer in India, who is typically engaged in unorganized sector, lacks formal professional qualification, has minimal education and earns approximately around INR 300,000 p.a. is an informed discretionary customer. He possesses basic facilities such as a rented accommodation either with a television set/refrigerator, a mobile phone per person with an average of five members per household in a city like Gurgaon, Haryana, India. For these items and other daily necessities like grocery, fruits, vegetables, and apparels, typically he spends 90 percent of his monthly household income. During the course of the study through constant comparison it emerged that "concern for family" forms the anchor point for all his purchase decisions which are basically utilitarian in nature. Money is a key constraint for him and he derives satisfaction or happiness on striking a deal which gives him a justification of benefits being received either more or equal to the price being charged. The functionality of the product weighed against the price charged constitutes value for him and he is willing to put extra physical effort and time to avail this value. He uses his judgment and discretion in deciding whether the product delivers on this functionality rather than being dependent on brand or distribution for this. Thus this equation of value received vs. value paid is what constitutes quality for him. His idea of value revolves around the core product and price being paid. But this customer does have his set of aspirations and sets his expectations along those, although presently he is satisfied much short of it because of the monetary constraint. Thus the resource endowment which may vary segment wise forms one of the core constructs for understanding satisfaction.

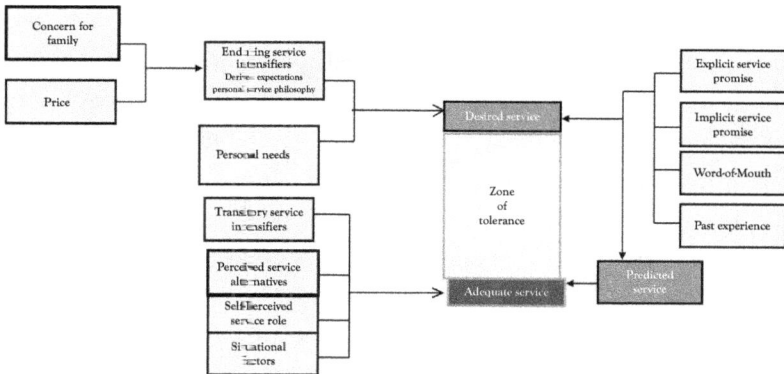

Figure 2.3 Integrated model of customer expectations for urban BoP customer in India

This substantive theory if integrated with the "zone of tolerance" model developed by Zeithaml, Parsuraman, and Berry 1993, which details how expectations are formed, would establish and elaborate *the role of concern for family and price* as drivers for both derived expectations and personal service philosophy in the Indian context. These stable factors work as enduring service intensifiers that sets the desired level of expectations in the zone of tolerance (Srivastava 2018).

Given the fact that this section represents a sizeable market and a sizeable population of India and with markets saturating and big market opportunity existing in the sector, it is important for firms to understand what satisfies him how does he make the purchase decision and what should be the focal point to differentiate. Satisfaction is the consumer's fulfillment response. It is a judgment that the product or service feature, or the product or service itself, provides a pleasurable level of consumption related fulfillment. It means satisfaction is the customer's evaluation of a market offering in terms of whether it meets the needs and expectations or not. Failures would lead to dissatisfaction. Thus it becomes imperative to understand what drives his expectation and accordingly satisfaction can be carved out. Satisfaction is closely linked to customer loyalty and firm profitability (Heskett, Sasser, and Schlesinger 1997). In such a case if we start understanding what satisfies an urban BOP customer and what is his idea of value; it can be deduced that his expectations revolve around concern for family and price and he derives value only in technical Service

Quality part that is the core benefit as contrasted with the functional service quality part within the SD logic based approach. But given that it is not that he does not expect or understand the functional Service Quality or the how part or it does not concern him at all. If made, it would be a wrong assumption that would be made.

The concern for family is different in different customer segments. At this point a very obvious question emerged as to how concern for family and price were different as drivers for customer expectations in purchase decision for the bottom of the pyramid segment than other segments. To answer this it was decided that instead of doing the same study with other segments if there was a product category which was used by some more customer segments and within that category if there was a product/brand that was purchased across segments, it could be seen as to what drives their purchase decisions against the urban bottom of the pyramid customer. Wheat flour or atta is one of the basic staples that forms the bulk of the Northern India cuisine. While earlier this was largely a commodity with no brands and packaged alternatives, presently there were FMCG companies that provided several alternatives in the market for packaged branded wheat flour; Hindustan Unilever's Annapurna, Patanjali, ITC Aashirvad to name a few. In urban North India ITC Aashirvad was the category leader. ITC was approached for the study and through interviews it was discussed with them as to what are the product attributes that they considered w.r.t. the customers. An interesting point was that while this brand was being purchased by customers in upper and middle income categories it was also being purchased by the lower income categories as they purchased from similar stores and were exposed to it through the households where they were employed. ITC typically focused on urban upper income categories and disclosed that they typically focused on health and lifestyle, packaging for a longer shelf life, purity and quality of wheat grains, taste, nutrition, storage, availability and convenience, processes that maintain the nutritional content. In fact the company did share the list of attributes and values but for the purposes of confidentiality it cannot be attached with the study. For the target segment for ITC in the branded wheat flour category the customer made the decision for family also but it was focused more on lifestyle dimensions based on psychographic factors leading to *Subjective Well Being* whereas the reasons for the Bottom of the Pyramid customer were price (the MRP vs. the quantity received), number of people the pack would feed across the number of days in the family, convenience, and aspiration. The main point of difference was that it was tilted more toward *Economic Well Being*, where money could be saved to fund the child education or a similar reason and decision was for the entire household, the upper income counterparts reflected more of individual decision making with influences from other family members.

As highlighted in the previous section through Grounded Theory it emerged that this customer is an informed customer whose expectations are anchored around family, constrained by price. It is only that coming from a collectivist culture and constrained by money *he does not see the functional service quality as a differentiator for which he would pay extra money* and many a times he is also exploited on this dimension as he is perceived to be powerless. But as markets mature in the other regions and segments, where businesses could draw a price premium for the functional quality component including developing markets because of the similarities in the customers businesses would turn to these BOP markets. *Their expectations will have to be understood differently as in the present to draw upon the Zone of tolerance and service quality implications* for this segment because the emphasis in the current times would be on this segment and it would be important for firms to handhold on existing needs to continue with them as they grow into the next segment. It is quite possible that *an integrated user based value definition of perceived service quality/ value may align well for this segment.*

A very important question arose at this point that the concern for family should probably already be addressed in the Consumer Behavior literature and it should be the same across income groups. While it is true that family has been studied widely and deeply in the Consumer Behavior literature, the basic orientation for family as a unit of analysis has been individuals and their influences within family rather than household as a unit of analysis which is the way this segment takes decision. This point has been detailed in Chapter 3.

Conclusion

Thus the following findings emerged from the study (Srivastava 2018):

- A *substantive theory that explains the purchase decision of the BOP Indian customer.*
- Integration with literature provides insight that this emergent substantive theory is the cornerstone of the BOP customer's personal beliefs in India that set the desired level in the zone of tolerance of his expectation.
- Additionally given his constraints on money and grounding in collectivist culture he would want the complete market offering comprising of both service quality and functional quality but it is the technical quality that would get more weightage whereas the other factors would work as hygiene factors.

The approach to this paper has been on elevating the focus of coding and analysis from the descriptive to the conceptual level and trusting one's intuitive sense of conceptualization. The reason for this has been that attributing meaning is not the goal of grounded theory rather grounded theory aims to offer the reader a conceptual application of a latent pattern of behavior that holds significance within the social setting under study.

CHAPTER 3

Delivering Customer Perceived Value at the Urban Bottom of the Pyramid in India

Introduction

After getting a fair idea of what constitutes value in the Urban Bottom of the Pyramid segment in India there is a need to adopt a delivery framework. This chapter details on the appropriate framework and its delivery mechanism.

One of the most popular mechanisms to deliver value by a firm, practiced and taught across business schools over the world is the, "Marketing Mix." It is commonly referred to as the 4Ps. The application of this framework is pervasive across business situations globally but it is an organization oriented framework that works from a decision-making perspective. There has been a need for a customer oriented marketing decision framework. This need is met by the "4As" framework developed by Sheth and Sisiodia (2012). It takes a customer oriented view in organizations and helps in thinking like a customer. The marketing mix 4Ps framework has been further modified for the services sector which considers 7Ps instead of 4Ps. The former was aligned to the goods dominant logic whereas the latter has been aligned to services dominant logic. The earlier 4Ps were; product, price, place, and promotion. The three additional Ps are People, Processes, and Physical Evidence. The Perceived Value construct has been conceptualized from the customer's view and thus it may be imperative to start the thought from the customer rather than the organization approaching the customer through different Ps. This is one of the limitations of the Marketing mix framework, even the extended one though the 7Ps are better customer aligned. The 4As thus serve the purpose better. The framework is first described in the following section and then adapted for delivering value in the bottom-of-the-pyramid segment.

The 4As framework starts by describing that in any marketplace transaction the customer plays different roles, typically four. The four roles are (Sheth and Sisiodia 2012);

- SEEKER: The customer seeks information about the product
- PAYER: The customer pays for it in terms of time, effort, and money
- BUYER: The customers select and acquire the product
- USER: The customers consume the product

It is possible that an individual or an organizational entity might play one or more of these roles in combination with other individuals or organizations. In a manner the customer's consumption of value does not happen as a whole but it is broken into parts. To consummate a sales all these parts have to be completed with full satisfaction of the entity playing that role. Marketing Managers must understand the difference between each role to deliver satisfactory value to the customer because each role lays emphasis on different aspects in a transaction. The authors of the framework highlight that the customers seek different market values from organizations based on the role that they are playing. It is important for companies to understand the values and characteristics that shape each role. There are different wants and desires that shape each role. The seeker may look for sufficient information about the offering. The users may focus on the product characteristics (such as efficiency, functionality, and reliability) apart from the experiential elements. For the payer the offering's total price is paramount. The buyer would desire a frictionless way to acquire the product. It is important to note that the seeker role is primarily associated with the "Awareness" of the offering, the user role deals with the "Acceptability" of that offering, the payer role relates to "Affordability" of the offering, and the buyer role deals with the "Accessibility" of the offering. In a business context the concept of buying center has prevailed which would include different departmental representatives playing these roles. There would be a user department, a finance department to decide the payment terms, people in procurement department who would be doing the process of purchase for the organization to illustrate a few. The authors further elaborate that in each role the customer seeks different values. It emerges that in each role the customer seeks two kinds of values as explained below. In the role of the user the values are performance and social. Each of the value defined in the original framework is being described as is;

- Performance Value refers to how effectively and consistently a product serves its principal function. It depends on the technical core of the product and thus depends on the quality of its design, engineering, and manufacturing.
- Social Value—Consumers purchase products not only for their physical characteristics but also for the social and emotional elements they provide. These could be sensory enjoyment, attainment of desired mood states, achievement of social and ego goals. Social value surfaces in products/brands that are perceived positively in important groups for the customer. Users for whom social value is important choose products that convey an image that they believe could help them fit in with a desired group or initiate new social relationships. Social value also considers market choices that arouse or satisfy an emotion.

Customers who are in the role of payers seek two important types of market values;

- Psychological: Psychological value of the customer refers to the consumer's willingness to pay the exchange price for what is being offered. When firms charge a premium on an offering the customer must perceive it to be fair. This would take into account the total costs incurred in acquiring the product.
- Economic Value: Customers not only have to be willing to pay the price asked but also be able to economically afford the price being asked. The availability of credit options is one

such strength that customers especially from the developing
economies value a lot.

As buyers, consumers are concerned with availability value and value
offered in convenience.

- Availability Value: Availability covers an adequate supply of
  the core offering along with the necessary accompanying
  services such as the pre and post purchase consultancy and
  help in keeping the product's usability. Many times marketers
  are able to build a strong demand but they are not able to
  close a deal because of the lack in supply. The reason for the
  gap could be poor sales forecasting, inadequate manufacturing
  capacity, a shortage of key components, transportation bottle-
  necks, or any other.
- Convenience Value: The customer must spend some amount
  of time and effort to acquire a product. The distance and time
  where the product must be made available must be customer
  friendly. The merchandise accessibility must also be according
  to the customer. The convenience value increases in proportion to the decrease in terms of consumer spend in time and
  effort.

Consumers in seeker's role seek happiness, fulfillment, satisfaction,
new and exciting experiences and solutions to the problems. People over
time continuously seek ways that would improve the quality of their lives.
Mature customers many a times look forward to meet higher order needs
such as self-actualization or enlightenment. Customers in seeker roles
continuously absorb information about product offering so that improves
the quality of their lives. Customers as seekers may be Active or Passive.
The seeker role has two dimensions: education and inspiration. The need
for education is to gain mastery over their work domain is very basic to
human beings as learning beings. Apart from this they also need inspiration; the spark to ignite their imagination which will help to consume
life in a novel and compelling manner. Inspiration is essential for customer to act on the information they gather. It is important to note that
the information technology revolution has changed the role of customers as seekers. Consumers today have stopped being passive recipients of

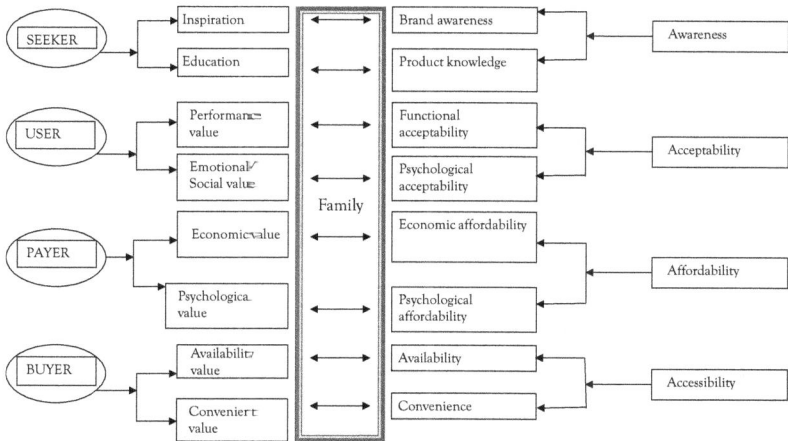

Figure 3.1 Customer roles and market values in the urban India BoP context (adapted from Sheth and Sisodia 2012).

poorly targeted information. The traditional mass media based marketing approaches do not fulfill the needs of customers as seekers. Interested customers are now active participants and content has to be designed in a specific manner to reach them. Marketers need to follow the 4As framework to satisfy the customers in each of the four roles. Before discussing the 4As framework in detail there is an important understanding related to the BOP context that needs to be incorporated.

As emerged through the grounded theory research and elaborated through the narratives in Chapter 2, the family dimension is very important for the Urban BOP Indian customers (Figure 3.1). The Urban BOP customer irrespective of the product category is satisfied through the family related need satisfaction. Irrespective of his role across product categories in the purchase decision, the decision is taken as a collective decision. This is a radical departure from the way marketing has traditionally viewed the customer in different roles and decision making with an individual orientation. The family/household is considered as the decision-making unit rather than the individual.

Sheth and Sisodia define the 4As as:

Awareness: The level to which the customers are informed of a product's characteristics, are persuaded to try it, and reminded to repurchase it. Awareness comprises of the following dimensions:

- Brand Awareness indicated by factors such as brand recall, associations, brand attraction, and perceived brand characteristic.
- Product Knowledge indicated by factors such as interest, understanding, involvement, and so on.

Acceptability: the level to which the firm's total product offering meets and exceeds the needs and expectations of customers in the target market. Acceptability is concerned about two dimensions:

- Functional Acceptability: covered by factors such as core attributes and capabilities, functionality, ease of use, quality, reliability, and so on.
- Psychological Acceptability: covered by points such as brand image indicated by reputation, positioning and personality, styling, social value, emotional value, perceived risk, and so on.

Affordability: the level of willingness that customers in the target market have to pay the product's price which includes both monetary and non-monetary price. It comprises of two dimensions:

- Economic Affordability: is the ability to pay which is indicated by factors such as income, time and effort required, assets, financing, fit within the budget
- Psychological Affordability: is the willingness to pay indicated by factors such as perceived value for money, perceived fairness, price relative to alternatives

Accessibility: the level to which customers are able to readily acquire and use the product. The two dimensions are:

- Availability: observed by factors such as supply relative to demand, products being stocked, related products and services
- Convenience: indicated by factors such as effort and time required to acquire a product, packaging in convenient sizes, and the ease to which the product can be found within and across locations

Measuring the 4As

The authors have provided immense help by not only providing the framework but also giving a measurement framework that is mentioned below.

For a firm to get the full advantage of the framework all the 4As must be measured and score high on all the 4As. Each of the A is measured on a 0–100 percent scale with respect to a given target market. The market value coverage (MVC) is calculated by considering each of As measured independently and then multiplied. The MVC serves as the measure of the effectiveness of the overall marketing program in ensuring the highest probability of the prospects being converted into actual customers. The four elements are not compensatory. They do not substitute each other rather a firm must do good on all the four dimensions to be successful and if it fails even in one dimension it will fail overall. Just to illustrate if the firm scores 100 percent on two dimensions but only 50 percent on the remaining two dimensions it will be able to achieve only 25 percent of its focused market (100*100*50*50). Similarly if all four dimensions are at 25 percent it will achieve only 0.39 percent. If it achieves zero in any one it will become zero in total. To achieve the market coverage at the Urban BOP in India the firm must create value in all the four areas that cut across the family dimension in different buying roles. If we start understanding customer perceived value from the customer angle it may be observed that the customer wants all; functional, social, hedonic, epistemic, and conditional value but all cutting through the family dimension. To achieve high MVC marketers must create value in all four areas. Customers do not expect trade-offs whereas Managers are often trading off.

During the grounded theory interviews the role of family as a collective unit emerged as being very important at the bottom of the pyramid segment in the urban India context. It is different from the way family context and family decision making have been studied in the marketing literature. The decision is not in terms of individual buyer roles but irrespective of the product category the decision itself is a collective household decision across product categories. By family the meaning is a system with average 5–6 family members that stay together in a single household premise. They share (resources) food, accommodation, and life together. The responsibilities are divided in terms of working adults in the age group of 25–60 years taking the responsibility of young children or elderly parents. Many times it is just the parents and the young children with grandparents in native village/town or it is the dependent parents living with adult working children. The decision making is different in a family above the bottom of the pyramid segment. The disposable income is a surplus resource as opposed to the BOP segment where it is a scarce resource and therefore there is quite latitude available in deciding how to spend and where to spend. Thus there could be a difference in the expectations and benefits from a purchase, the way roles exercise themselves in decision making, communication would be different and firm's marketing strategies may also be different. All this will lead to a difference in customer perceived value and satisfaction derived through or after the purchase.

It is thus worthwhile to understand the concept of family as studied in the research literature of buyer behavior in Marketing before understanding its placement in the customer's perceived value equation, specifically in the context of urban Indian BOP customer. Family as a consuming and decision making unit have remained a central phenomenon in the marketing domain but research has largely focused on a few aspects about family decision making while several of them have been left. The focus has been largely on questions such as (Commuri and Gentry 2000):

- Who decides?
- What are the consumption implications of women in labor force?
- Can the relative influence of husbands and wives be determined?
- Does the family lifecycle matter?

There are issues in the family dynamics beyond these which impacts their behavior. These behavioral responses are important for the customers. The restrictive idea of family in consumption decisions need to be removed and one such idea is "customer perceived value." Family research has largely focused on decision outcomes in terms of who makes the final decision rather than on decision processes (how do they arrive at decisions). Secondly, most theories in psychology on behavior and personality touch behaviors at individual level and if family is not a sum of individuals, individual theories of behavior and personality do not facilitate an explanation of behavior observed in families.

Most of the family research has been on decision roles—who makes what decisions? Since 1955 when the research on this topic began it centered on the role of husband and wife in decision making across a diverse set of product categories. The study has been adapted with a shift in decision role stages by Cunningham and Green (1974) and the kind of decisions; joint, syncretic, and autonomic in family decision behavior (Davis and Rigaux 1974). Research has also focused on decision role structure across decisions. It was found that husbands dominated decisions for certain product categories and wives for some (Belch et al. 1985) but the focus of most of the studies was on individual decisions. It was also debated that decision roles studied were over simplified. Responses from one spouse may not be sufficient to understand the roles and family decisions. Researchers explored the possibility of a multidimensional definition of power and influence (Davis 1971, 1976; Davis and Rigaux 1974). It was suggested that the entire decision-making process was relooked (Wilkes 1975).

Subsequent research paid attention to the determinants of relative influence and thus to the decision roles; for illustration Rosen and Granbois (1983) found that sex role attitudes (whether traditional or not) and education were the most relevant determinants. Parallel to some feminist work in the area of women's employment, Rosen and Granbois reported that the reason for the wife's employment was also a critical factor in determining role structure. Joag, Gentry, and Ekstrom (1991) developed a role/goal model of wife decision making that incorporated both work status and motivation for working.

As highlighted by the authors the subject of relative influence can be considered as a subset of decision roles. The outcome of a decision may be equally satisfying to both husband and wife but for different reasons. The authors write that the nature of the decision gets complicated because of the involvement of more than two players in decision making. There was a need for a multi-dimensional typology to understand family decision making as there could be misperceptions related to joint decision making. Park 1982 suggested that the process of joint decision making was one in which couples muddled rather than steered according to a predetermined strategy. The emphasis on conflict resolution as the driving force through each stage and the classification of product attributes in terms of their role in resolution of conflicts was an important area for understanding of marketing researchers. The role of couples and their children has also been studied and the underlying causes of differences in relative influence also remain unexplained (Filiatrault and Ritchie 1980).

As per the authors much of the relative influence research has apparently been conducted from a competitive perspective implying an either-or kind of mentality on the part of the spouses. Qualls 1988 states, "influence is defined in the present study as the perception of one action taken by one spouse to obtain his or her most preferred decision outcome while simultaneously stopping the attainment of their spouses' most preferred outcomes." A cooperative perspective might look harder for implicit as opposed to explicit measures of influence. Such a perspective would suggest that many family decisions do not constitute only conscious choice, but also incorporate a shared consensus, mutual trust, and the desire to maintain harmony. Sillars and Karbflesch 1987 conclude that implicit adjustment does not occur smoothly. Further, highly implicit transactions are limited to more homogenous and stable relationships where the shared experience of individuals allows them to fill in considerable taken-for-granted feeling.

Since concern for family emerges an important dimension in the purchase behavior of the urban Indian BOP customer and this segment presents market opportunity it is important for firms to understand what satisfies this customer, how does he make the purchase decision and what should be the focal point to differentiate. This point has been detailed in Chapter 2.

BOP in Other Family Contexts

In line with the idea of researching the "how" of family decision making rather than "who" the Chapter 2 narrative interviews in detail explore that. It is important to understand how family has been understood in other contexts also. There is not much literature available though on the subject with reference to the bottom of the pyramid customer context. Authors Chickweche, Stanton, and Fletcher (2012) studied the family purchase decision making at the bottom of the pyramid in the context of Zimbabwe. The study nature and findings being close to the subject of the book makes it worthwhile to be mentioned. The authors explain how the makeup of the family and its role in individual lives vary from market to market as observed in the Western or Emerging or BOP markets. The concept and definition of family itself would be different in the latter two contexts. The western markets focus on the nuclear family comprising of father, mother, and siblings. The BOP markets are more likely to extend the concept of extended family comprising of nuclear family plus relatives. In the context of urban BOP in India the family may be living in two parts/two locations; the nuclear one in the city and grandparents (father's side) in the village or hometown. This in no case implies that western markets do not have the concept of extended family but the proportion and scope varies. "Family" has been acknowledged in the management literature yet the literature is largely derived from the developed markets. The emerging markets still have to be understood in detail, differences in the Eastern and Western philosophies could reflect in the structure of the family, their roles and decision-making processes. The family purchase decision also has to be understood in different markets under differing environmental constraints. As already acknowledged through the literature on family behavior of different themes the ones pertinent to be studied at BOP important ones could be roles, what factors lead led to adoption of these buyer roles and can an individual play multiple role, gender influence on roles, sex orientation in different kinds of individuals, joint and autonomic decision, nature of products under purchase (low involvement/high involvement). The research majorly considers all these under high involvement context but assumes that low involvement being habitual purchases does not require joint decision making. The western developed markets may hold this but the BOP markets do not agree to it because for them every decision is a joint decision as a result of income constraint. Wiliams and Burns (2000) advise to expand the scope of investigations. The potential impact of economic and social constraints also needs to be considered. The role of children also needs to be looked closely with reference to decision making in BOP markets. The impact of gender and spousal changes may also vary between Developed and BOP markets,

The authors cite that Zimbabwe is a BOP market that has been subjected to policy induced risks which has created social conflict, political instability, and economic mismanagement which is found in many emerging economies. In Zimbabwe this created population movements and gave rise to different BOP groups referred to as diluted urban, urban based, rural-urban based, and rural based. While such a classification is not available in India the study used the Unitus Ventures' pyramid to identify the urban BOP. The profile of the customers has been highlighted in Chapter 2. The authors in the Zimbabwean context followed a mixed method research with interviews and focus groups drawn from all the four groups. However, the Indian study concentrated only on Urban BOP typically residing in metros, working in the informal sector comprising both locals and immigrants. The data for Zimbabwean study was collected between 2006 and 2008. Apart from focus group discussions and qualitative customer interviews, ethnographic observations were also done. The techniques permitted multiple sources of information from multiple approaches, a kind of triangulation. The authors also lived with the informants in their environments to enrich the insights. Since the food and personal hygiene products from 65 percent of the purchase basket of the customers in Zimbabwe, these categories were chosen for the purchase decision. Random purposive sampling was done to improve the credibility of the sample. The text data was analyzed using condensation, categorization, narration, interpretation, and ad hoc approaches. Condensation reduced the text to succinct summaries. Categorization reduced the data to categories, figures, and tables. Narrative structuring was done by creating a coherent structure and plots of data. A re-contextualization of the statements within a broader framework of reference from literature was done for interpretation of the text. NVIVO software was used for the analysis of the data. The findings of the study are reported only for the urban BOP customers in Zimbabwe followed by a comparison with the Indian urban BOP.

The family structure of this group comprised of a husband as the head of the family comprising of his wife and children. The concept of family included extended family typically living in rural areas. This characteristic is common for the Indian urban BOP. A very unique and prominent characteristic was that every purchase was deemed to be important by the customer. Thus food and personal hygiene were important and high involvement categories for them. Under the condition of limited income each time they had to make sure whether they were purchasing right. The categories were considered to be complex decision categories. This condition is similar to India. Because of the economic conditions there were three types of purchase behavior reflected in the group; buying products as and when available, or when needed, or when they could afford them. Product categories were normal which forced them to purchase products as and when they found them. An important finding was the tendency to make sacrifices by these consumers to buy products at times when they did not have the money to do so. This was done for two reasons:

1.   Ready availability of the products
2.   To take advantage of value in price terms

Both these characteristics are common to the Indian urban BOP.

Differences in family decision models have been explained in the study using the consumer roles theory of initiator, decider, buyer, user, and gatekeeper. However, through the research gaps it is now relevant that family decision models are also explored through other means and beyond this framework only. Traditionally, across the globe women had an overriding role in the purchase of food and personal hygiene with husband and children being the user. But there was a change in the urban BOP segments where husbands and wives shared the responsibility of purchasing the products in these categories. The gender-based approach had changed. Any one of the two who found the products at cheaper prices. While the approach is observed in India as well yet here the decision is most of the time joint in nature even at the start of it. All factors are shared and concerned at the beginning itself.

In the Zimbabwean study (figure 3.2) because of the economic conditions the focus was price and thus anyone who found a better deal initiated the purchase. This behavior was different from India where the discussion started prior to the purchase and it was decided as to who

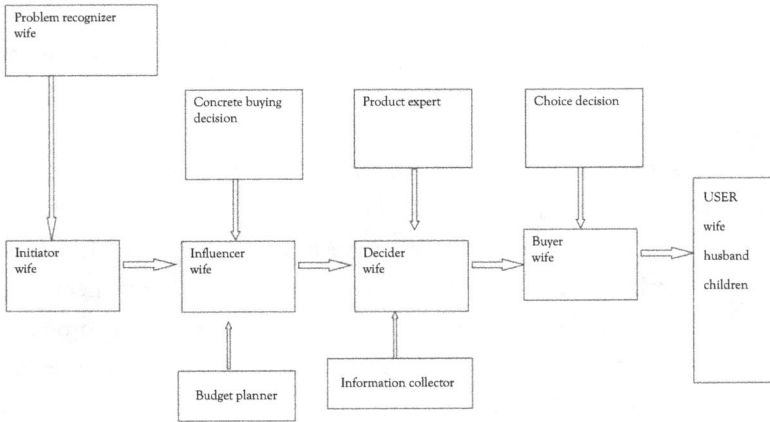

Figure 3.2 Adapted from Jensen 1990

would start that as well. The study noted that the husband was more responsible for purchase in the shared gender role but there was no consensus amongst the participants who also considered women playing an important role. It was a similar situation as in India.

The role of children reflected their little influences at the younger ages in product categories such as food and personal hygiene. The influence was observed to be stronger in the categories with children in later stages of the family lifecycle where they became responsible for buying their parent's personal food and hygiene products. Multiple roles of children in the purchase decision were evident where adult children were responsible for the support of their parents and siblings. This group called the "working children" assumed the roles of decision makers, influencers, and purchasers of actual products. Many a times the decisions were initiated by the parents with the children, where ultimately the call was taken on availability and price with users including everyone in the family. The findings were similar in nature to India. While the Zimbabwean study did not reflect the influence of children in different age groups, in India the role of the children till adolescence was largely of users rather than influencers. The role only changed when they started earning and became an income generating resource for the family, where they started playing the role of the decision maker or influencer which was also minimal. Only when they reached the ages of 20–22 years or assumed larger role and responsibility in running the family that their weightage in the decision

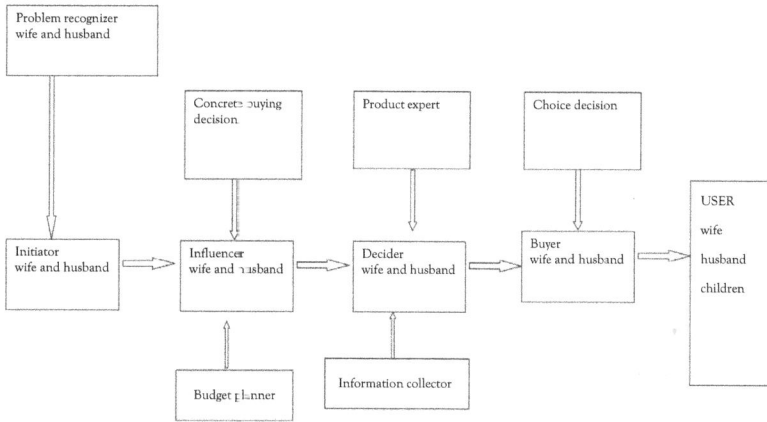

Figure 3.3 Adapted from Jensen 1990

whether as decision maker or influencer changed. It is important to note that the role of an individual in the family and the responsibility attached decided the role in the purchase decision irrespective of age.

Because of the tough economic environment interviews from the urban BOP who wanted to consider the influence of their children in the purchase decision were not able to do so. This is similar to the Indian case where money is an important decision constraint. This is unlike the higher income groups which can accommodate the children's concern in the decision.

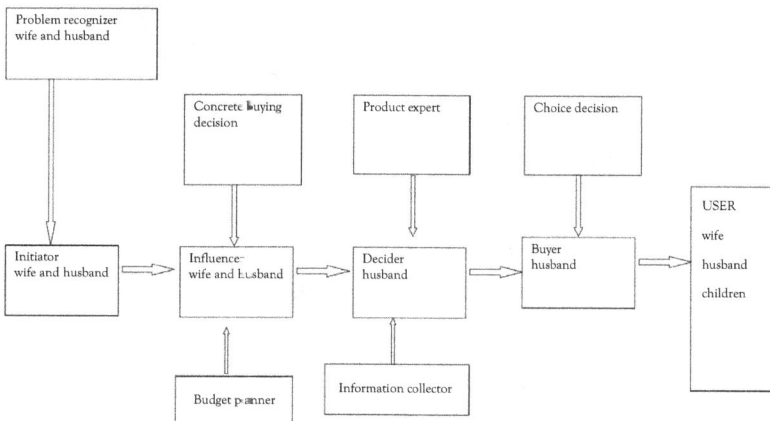

Figure 3.4 Adapted from Jensen 1990

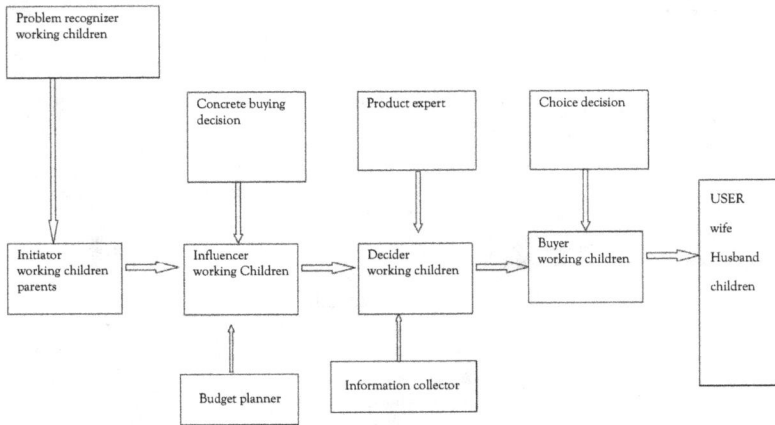

Figure 3.5 Adapted from Jensen 1990

The findings of the study (Figures 3.2 to 3.5) and its contrast with India highlight the importance of doing such studies by academicians and practitioners. The main reason is that there is a need for marketers to understand the heterogeneity of the BOP market and the dynamics of the family purchase decision process that takes place and is different from the western developed counterparts where both practice and theory have been developed. Marketing models needs to incorporate the different roles played by men, women, and children in the purchase decision process and accounting as value for them. It is important for suppliers to understand the relevance of social networks and buying groups for the BOP consumers and design distribution systems accordingly. The appropriateness of such distribution system to the marketing environment is important. These social systems are then further used for such marketing activities such as marketing communications.

Evolution and Contextualization of Customer Perceived Value

In Chapter 1, the concept of value was discussed. It is again being revisited in slightly more detail to understand different conceptual perspectives briefly followed by the way it has been measured. Table 3.1 presents

Table 3.1 Select definitions of customer perceived value

Source/year	definition
Zeithaml (1988)	Value is the consumer's overall assessment of the utility of a product based on perceptions of what is received and what is given. Value denotes the conceptual trade-off framework of what is received and what is given. Four diverse meanings of value that were identified are: value is low price; value is whatever one wants in a product; value is the quality that the consumer receives for the price paid; value is what the consumer gets for what he or she gives. It describes the post-consumption value. The components (benefit and sacrifice) are covered in the dimensions given
Day (1990)	Perceived customer value is the surplus between customer's perceived benefits and customer's perceived costs Perceived customer value= customer's perceived benefits– customer's perceived costs
Monroe (1990)	Buyers' perceptions of value represent a trade-off between the quality and benefits they perceive in the product relative to the sacrifice they perceive by paying the price
Urbany and Bearden (1989)	Perceived acquisition value is the buyers' net gain (or trade-off) from acquiring the product or service
Lichtenstein, Netemeyer, and Burton (1990)	Perceived transaction value is the perception of psychological satisfaction or pleasure obtained from taking advantage of the financial terms of the price deal
Dodds et al. (1991)	Perceived customer value is the ratio of perceived benefits relative to perceived sacrifice
Anderson, Jain, and Chintagupta (1993)	Value in business markets is the perceived worth in monetary units of the set of economic, technical, service, and social benefits received by a customer firm in exchange for the price paid for a product, taking into consideration the available suppliers' offerings and prices
Gale (1994)	Customer value is market perceived quality which is adjusted for the relative price of the products. It is your customer's opinion of your products/services as compared to that of your competitors
Holbrook (1996)	Value is "an interactive relativistic preference experience." Value is interactive because it involves an interaction between some subject and some object. It is relativistic because it is comparative (among objects), personal (across consumers), and situational (specific to the context in which the evaluative judgment occurs). It is concerned with the consumption experience resulting from the use of an object or the appreciation of an object

(Continued)

Table 3.1 Select definitions of customer perceived value (Continued)

Source/year	definition
'Ravald and Gronroos (1996)	Value is considered to be an important constituent of relationship marketing and the ability of a company to provide superior value to its customers is regarded as one of the most successful strategies for the 1990s. This ability has become a means of differentiation and a key to the riddle of how to find a sustainable competitive advantage

Source: Adapted from Kainth, J.S., and Verma, H.V. 2011. "Consumer Perceived value: Construct Apprehension and its Evolution." *Journal of Advanced Social Research*, no. 1, pp. 20–57.

the select definitions of customer perceived value as reviewed by Kainth and Verma (2011).

While studying the literature the most comprehensive work done on perceived value was observed to be done of Sheth, Newmann and Gross (1991). The authors studied 650 papers across disciplines that included economics, sociology, different relevant branches of psychology, marketing, and consumer behavior. The authors have not called their theory as theory of perceived value but what they write is on understanding the consumption values in a purchase decision. The theory focused on consumption values explaining why consumers choose to buy or not buy, use or not use a particular product, the reasons for consumers to choose one particular product type over another and one brand over another. The authors have tested the theory in the context of consumers considering smoking and the decision to purchase or not purchase, use or not use cigarettes, the choice of one cigarette over another and the choice of one cigarette brand over another. Although there has been research on perceived value after that as illustrated from the table yet this is a seminal work that has set the direction in the literature. Other researchers have used it extensively to develop the thought.

Taking the work of Sheth et al. before defining the consumption values the three propositions on which the theory rests are:

1. Consumer choice is a function of multiple consumption values.
2. The consumption values make differential contribution in any given choice situation.
3. The consumption values are independent.

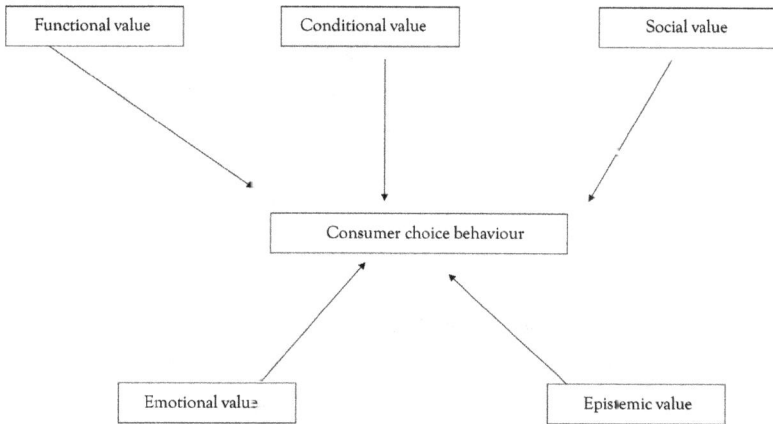

Figure 3.6 Values influencing consumer choice, adapted from Sheth, J.N., Newman, B.I. and Gross, B.L. 1991. *Consumption Values and Market Choice.* **South Western Publishing Company, Cincinnati, OH.**

The theory has identified five consumption choice behaviors (Figure 3.6). Research of customer values has used this theory in different context, while this remains at the base. The values discovered are functional, social, emotional, epistemic, and conditional. Each value is now described in detail.

Functional Value: Sheth et al. quote the functional value of an alternative as, "the perceived utility" acquired from an alternative's capacity for functional, utilitarian, or physical performance. An alternative acquires functional value through the possession of salient functional, utilitarian, or physical attributes. Functional value is measured on a profile of choice attributes. The functional value has traditionally been held as the prime driver of consumer choice. It supports the economic utility theory (Marshall 1890; Stigler 1950) that popularly finds expression as "rational economic man." An offering's functional value may also be decided by its characteristics or attributes such as reliability, durability, and price.

Social Value: the authors have defined social value as, "the perceived utility acquired from an alternative's association with one or more social groups." An alternative acquires social value through association with positively or negatively stereotyped demographic, socioeconomic, and cultural ethnic groups. Social value is measured on a profile of choice imagery. The authors write that choices involving highly visible products such as clothing, jewelry to be shared with others are often goods/services driven by social value. The authors have considered social value by researching theories in other areas. The notable ones amongst those are Warner and Lunt's (1941) work on social class, Hyman (1942) work on reference group, Rogers (1962) work on diffusion of innovations, Veblen (1899) work on conspicuous consumption, and Robertson's (1967) work on social values with respect to consumer choice as a result of interpersonal communication and information.

Emotional Value: the authors have defined emotional value as the perceived utility acquired from an alternative's capacity to arouse feelings or affective states. An offering acquires emotional value when associated with specific feelings or when precipitating or perpetuating those feelings. Emotional value is measured on a profile of feelings associated with the alternative.

Goods and services have been associated often with emotional response. Emotional value has been associated thus with aesthetic alternatives however they are applicable to tangible products as well. The authors have conceptualized emotional value based on motivation research carried by Dichter (1947) that elaborated how consumer choice can be driven by noncognitive and unconscious motives. The authors have also considered the research in atmospherics and advertising regarding how marketing and promotional mix variables arouse emotional responses that can be attributed to marketed products (Martineau 1958; Zajonac 1968; Kotler 1974; Holbrook 1983; Park and Young 1986). The nonverbal information processing that works on hemispherical brain lateralization (Orstein 1972; Hansen 1981) which addresses the specialized functioning of the two sides of human brain for both verbal and pictorial information.

Epistemic Value: the epistemic value has been defined by the authors as the perceived utility acquired from the alternatives' capacity to arouse curiosity, provide novelty and satisfy a desire for knowledge. An offering acquires epistemic value by referring to items of curiosity, novelty, and knowledge. When a customer is bored or saturated with the existing offering, or is curious or has a desire to learn then the change of pace/change of experience or a totally new experience will provide him with epistemic value. The research on epistemic value has considered different kinds of exploratory, novelty seeking, and variety seeking behaviors of customers for activating product search, trial, and switching behaviors (Katz and

Lazarsfeld 1955; Howard and Sheth 1969; Hansen 1972; Hirschman 1980). Berlyne's (1960, 1970) works on optimal stimulation and arousal has been included where he contends that individuals are driven to maintain an optimal or intermediate level of stimulation. Customer innovativeness or a consumer's propensity to adopt new products has been incorporated as conditional value (Rogers and Shoemaker 1971; Hirschman 1980).

Conditional Value: the authors define conditional value as "the perceived utility acquired by an alternative as the result of a specific situation or circumstances facing the choice maker. An offering acquires conditional value in the presence of antecedent physical or social contingencies that increase its functional or social value. Conditional value is measured on a profile of choice contingencies." The authors state that the offering's utility would depend on the situation. Products often have situation based associations such as popcorns and movies.

The five values identified make differential contributions in different choice contexts and they are proposed as independent values, adding relatively and contributing incrementally to customer choice. Further customer perceived value has been identified as an antecedent for creating customer satisfaction, repurchase intention, and loyalty (Linetal 2015). Apart from the Sheth et al. work on consumption values, customer perceived value has been conceptualized by other researchers. It is relevant to understand how research has considered customer perceived value in terms of dimensions.

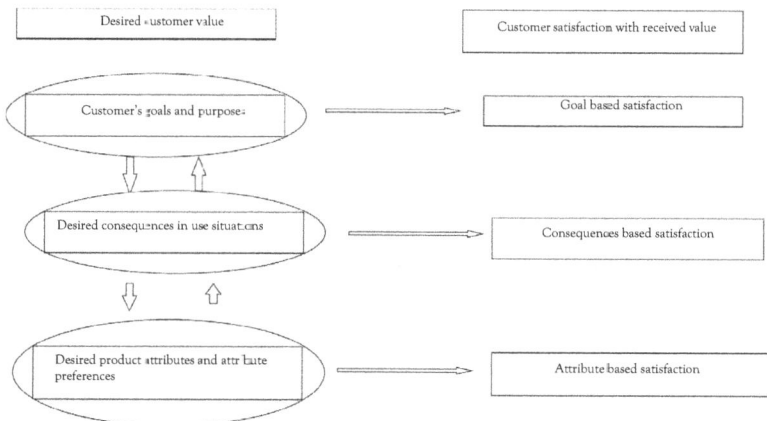

Figure 3.7 Value hierarchy model of customer perceived value

Value Hierarchy Model

Septa et al. (2016) write that according to this model (Figure 3.7) customer desired value has been divided into three levels; desired attributes, desired consequences, and desired end states referred to as goals.

Given by Woodruff (1997) this model defines CPV as customer's perceived preference for an evaluation of those product attributes, attribute performances and consequences arising from use that facilitate or block achieving the customer's goals and purpose in use situations.

Utilitarian and Hedonic Model

This approach talks of customer perceived value being dichotomous in nature; utilitarian and hedonic, that is, a firm's product would be valued on the basis of its performance or functions along with the experience that customers would get in the product consumption. The latter would include symbolic and hedonic aspect. Only the three broad research directions in value have been mentioned to help the reader understand the boundary line through different streams taken in academic research. The commonalities in definitions are around the components of value that form the major themes (Table 3.2).

Within the broad gamut researchers have worked on different dimensions of value along with their anchor as listed in Tables 3.3 and 3.4.

Most of the dimensions studied are classified either on the benefits side or sacrifices side. It is important to note that these studies have not taken the environmental setting into account. Except for some isolated studies there has been no integration of BOP perceived value in literature although it is such an important segment.

Measuring Customer Perceived Value

Till now we focused on the conceptualization customer perceived value as done in research. It is equally important to concentrate on the measurement aspect as well. Most of the researchers have taken the approach as outlined by Sheth et al. 1991 for their study. For operationalizing the

Table 3.2 Commonalities in value definitions

Components	Source/year
Combination of all factors qualitative and quantitative; objective and subjective to form a consumer's buying experience	Schechter (1984) cited in Zeithaml (1988)
Interaction between some subject and some object	Holbrook (1996)
Situational	Holbrook (1996)
	Woodruff (1997)
Trade-off between what is received (benefit) and what is given (sacrifice)	Zeithaml (1988)
	Day (1990)
	Monroe (1990)
	Urbany and Bearden (1989)
	Dodds et al. (1991)
	Anderson, Jain, and Chintagupta (1993)
	Gale (1994)
	Cronin, Brady, Brand, Hightower, and Shemwell (1997)
	Woodruff (1997)
	Patterson and Spreng (1997)
Cognition	Zeithaml (1988)
	Woodruff (1997)
	Patterson and Spreng (1997)
Emotional/psychological/pleasure	Lichtenstein, Netemeyer, and Burton (1990)
Business markets	Anderson, Jain, and Chintagupta (1993)
Competition	Anderson, Jain, and Chintagupta (1993)
	Gale (1994)
	Ravald and Gronroos (1996)
Relationship marketing	Ravald and Gronroos (1996)
	Butz and Goodstein (1996)
	Sirdeshmukh, Singh, and Sabol, (2002)
Goals and purposes	Woodruff (1997)

Source: Adapted from Kainth, J.S., and Verma, H.V. 2011. "Consumer Perceived Value: Construct Apprehension and Its Evolution." *Journal of Advanced Social Research* 1, no. 1, pp. 20–57.

Table 3.3 Value dimensions

Year	Source	Dimensions	Explanation of dimension
1988	Zeithaml	1. Intrinsic attributes (benefits)	How the purchase makes you feel
		2. Extrinsic attributes (benefits)	Reputation of the product or service
		3. Perceived quality (benefits)	The utility derived from the expected performance of the product
		4. Price (sacrifice)	It is the perceived sacrifice involved. It includes both monetary and nonmonetary considerations
1991	Sheth, Newman, and Gross	1. Functional value	The perceived utility acquired from an alternative's capacity for functional, utilitarian, or physical performance. It is measured on a profile of choice attributes. Generally the prime driver. Assumes economic utility theory and rationality. It is derived from the characteristics and attributes of an alternative
		2. Social value	The perceived utility acquired from an alternative's association with one or more specific social groups (demographic, socioeconomic and cultural-ethnic). It is a major driving force in highly visible products because of the demonstration effect
		3. Emotional value	The perceived utility acquired from an alternative's capacity to arouse feelings or affective states. It is often associated with aesthetic alternatives
		4. Epistemic value	The perceived utility acquired from an alternative's capacity to arouse curiosity, provide novelty, and satisfy a desire for knowledge. It is generally associated with entirely new experiences
		5. Conditional value	The perceived utility acquired from an alternative as the result of the specific situation or set of circumstances facing the choice maker
1991	Dodds, Monroe, and Grewal	1. Perceived acquisition value	Perceived acquisition value is the buyers' net gain (or trade-off) from acquiring the product or service

Year	Source	Dimensions	Explanation of dimension
1998	Grewal, Monroe, and Krishnan	2. Perceived transaction value	Perceived transaction value is the perception of psychological satisfaction or pleasure obtained from taking advantage of the financial terms of the price deal
1994	Babin, Darden, and Griffin (PSV (Personal Shopping Value) scale assumes Consumption Values by Sheth, Newman, and Gross(1991)	1. Hedonic value	It is a festive and joyous side of shopping. It is more subjective and personal. It reflects shopping's potential entertainment and emotional worth. It helps in explaining: impulsive purchases (results from the need to purchase than a need for a product) and compulsive purchases (where shoppers gain intrinsic value from the act of purchasing itself)
		2. Utilitarian value	It results from some type of conscious pursuit of an intended consequence. It is considered task related and rational. It reflects shopping with a work mentality
1995	Naumann	1. Place	Concerned with attributes like location, layout, design and parking facilities, and so on
		2. Product	Concerned with attributes of quality, branding and all
		3. Service	Concerned with attributes like accessibility, check out facility, and so on
		4. People	Concerned with attributes like knowledge, courtesy and staffing, and so on
		5. Communication	Concerned with attributes like
		6. Image	It is about reputation of the supplier
		7. Price	Actual price against which the customer compares the performance to form value perceptions
1995	Groth	1. Cognitive: perceived utility	It refers to the utility derived from the functional aspect of the product or service
		2. Psychological	The utility derived from the feelings or affective states that a product/service generates
		3. Internal	Internal values, such as self-fulfillment and self-respect imply that the individual believes that he or she can control value fulfillment

(Continued)

Table 3.3 Value dimensions (Continued)

Year	Source	Dimensions	Explanation of dimension
		4. External	External values, such as being well-respected and sense of belonging emphasize fulfillment beyond the control of the individual
1996	Holbrook	1. Extrinsic/ utilitarian	Consumption is appreciated for its function and utility
		2. Intrinsic/ hedonic	Consumption experience is treated as an end in itself
		3. Self-oriented	Consumer appreciates a product/experience for his own sake, for how he reacts to it and the effect it has on him
		4. Other oriented	Consumer looks beyond self to others such as family, friends and country, and so on
		5. Active	Involves any physical or mental manipulation of intangible or tangible object by an Individual
		6. Passive	Results from responding to objects. It arises from things done to an individual
1996	Kantamneni and Coulson	1. Societal value	It is clearly representative of societal value: accrued when the product is useful, ethically produced and benefits the society
		2. Experiential value	It shows the senses: if the product smells, feels, looks and sounds good, then the product has more value
		3. Functional value	It is purely functional value in the sense that products should be reliable, safe and functional, that is, provide the core benefit for which it is bought
		4. Market value	It is indicative of market value: a high priced product, with a good brand name and bought in a good or upscale store will have more value
1997	Gronroos	1. Cognitive	It refers to the utility derived from the functional aspect of the product or service
		2. Emotional (psychological)	The utility derived from the feelings or affective states that a product/service generates
1997	De Ruyter, Wetzels, Lemmink, and Mattson	1. Emotional dimension or intrinsic value	Intrinsic value represents the affective appreciation of the process of a service episode, regardless of the actual outcome. It pertains to the emotional side of a service delivery process

Year	Source	Dimensions	Explanation of dimension
		2. Functional dimension or extrinsic value	Extrinsic value pertains to the utilitarian aspects of a service episode, that is, a service episode as a useful means to a certain end
		3. Systematic value	Systemic value concerns the inherent relation between concepts in their systematic interaction, for example, the relationship between sacrifices and returns. It concentrates on rational or logical aspects of a service episode
1999	Sweeney, Soutar, and Johnson	1. Social value (acceptability)	The utility derived from the product's ability to enhance self concepts
		2. Emotional value	The utility derived from the feelings or affective states that a product generates
		3. Functional value (price/ value for money)	The utility derived from the product due to its perceived short term and longer-term costs
		4. Functional value (performance/quality)	The utility derived from the perceived quality and expected perceived quality and expected performance of the product
		5. Functional value (versatility)	The utility derived from the versatility and practicality of the product
2000	Hall et al.	1. Emotional/ social value	Emotional value: The utility derived from the feelings or affective states that a product generates. Social value (acceptability): The utility derived from the product's ability to enhance self concepts. Sweeney (1996) divided these two values; however, this study shows the two as so closely intertwined that they should be considered as one
		2. Perceived risk	A factor, which is not addressed by Sweeney (1996), is perceived risk; this study shows that for intangible products, factors reducing risk are highly sought
		3. Functional price	The utility derived from the product due to its perceived short term and longer-term costs
		4. Functional Quality	The utility derived from the perceived quality and expected perceived quality and expected performance of the product

(Continued)

Table 3.3 Value dimensions (Continued)

Year	Source	Dimensions	Explanation of dimension
2000	Williams, Soutar	1. Functional value	Perceived utility acquired from an alternative's capacity for functional, utilitarian or physical performance, (Sheth, Newman, and Gross 1991a, p. 160); prominent in pre-consumption stage
		2.Emotional value	The ability of the product or service to arouse feelings or affective states (Sheth, Newman, and Gross 1991). Prominent in post-consumption stage
		3.Social value	Perceived utility acquired from an alternative's association with one or more specific social groups, (Sheth, Newman, and Gross 1991a, p. 161)
		4. Epistemic value	The perceived utility acquired when the product arouses curiosity, provides novelty, and satisfies a desire for knowledge (Sheth, Newman, and Gross 1991a, p. 162)
2000	Parasuraman and Grewal	1. Acquisition value	It emphasizes the net gains associated with the benefits and the money given for acquiring and using a product or service
		2. Transaction value	Refers to the psychological satisfaction or pleasure obtained by purchasing the product at a good price compared to customer's internal reference price
		3. In-use value	It means utility derived from using the product or service
		4. Redemption value	It relates to benefits of service termination
2001	Sweeney and Soutar PERVAL	1. Emotional	The utility derived from the feelings or affective states that a product generates
		2. Social	The utility derived from the product's ability to enhance social self-concept
		3. Quality/performance	The utility derived from the perceived quality and expected performance of the product
		4. Price/value	The utility derived from the product due to the reduction of its perceived short term and longer-term costs

Year	Source	Dimensions	Explanation of dimension
2002	Petrick SERVPERVAL	1. Quality	Consumer's judgment about a product or service's overall excellence or superiority (Zeithaml 1988)
		2. Emotional response	Descriptive judgment regarding the pleasure that a product or service gives the purchaser (Sweeney et al. 1998)
		3. Monetary price	Price of a service as encoded by the consumer (Jacoby and Olson 1977)
		4. Behavioral price	Price (nonmonetary) of obtaining a service, which included the time and effort, used to search for the service (Zeithaml 1988)
		5. Reputation	Prestige or status of a product or service, as perceived by the purchaser, based on the image of the supplier (Docds et al. 1991)
2003	Woodall	1. Net Value for Customer (VC)	The balance of benefits and sacrifices: (the customer makes some judgment on the "worth whileness" of a product/service by computing or comparing weights and "quantities" of benefits and sacrifices
		2. Marketing VC	The perceived product attributes: (VC conceived as "product attributes")
		3. Derived VC	Use/experience outcomes: (VC here is conceptualized as the benefits derived from consumption-related experience and are presented as independent of any sense of associated sacrifice)
		4. Sale VC	Option determined primarily on price: (VC conceived as a reduction in sacrifice, or low price)
		5. Rational VC	Difference between the estimated and the objective price: (Dependent upon the perceived benefits or attributes of the product under consideration, the customer calculates what a "fair" price might be in relation to the benchmark(s) already established. VC in this context is the difference between the two, stated in a relevant currency)
2003	Minna Pura	1. Functional value	Functional value is related to either monetary benefits or convenience and the mobile service is either perceived better than alternative services or it increases freedom from technology

(Continued)

Table 3.3 Value dimensions (Continued)

Year	Source	Dimensions	Explanation of dimension
		2. Social value	Refer to hedonic aspects of consumption (e.g., enjoyment and other feelings), that is, mobile services can be used for fun. Social value is derived through reputation
		3. Emotional value	Refer to hedonic aspects of consumption (e.g., enjoyment and other feelings), that is, mobile services can be used for fun. Emotional value is gained by emotion-laden communication (positive or negative)
		4. Conditional value	Conditional value is a parallel category to other value categories that may increase or decrease the value perceptions
2004	Heinoen	1. Technical value	It denotes the characteristics of the core service and the service provider. Subdimensions—service characteristics; price; tangibles and image
		2. Functional value	Relates to an evaluation of functional aspects of the service delivery process. It denotes how the service interaction process occurs, that is, the "how" component. It involves the input and output of the service process. Subdimensions—Customer input; impact; process and company input
		3. Temporal value	Is based on temporal aspects affecting value perceptions. It represents how the customer perceives the temporal flexibility relating to when the service interaction occurs. It shows the "when" component, that is, ability to choose the time of the service delivery. Sub dimensions—time use and temporal latitude
		4. Spatial value	Is spatially driven and related to the usage location. It denotes how the customer perceives the spatial flexibility relating to where the service interaction occurs. It denotes the "where" component, that is, ability to choose the location of the service delivery. Subdimensions—spatial latitude; space; appearance; spatial inconvenience

Source: Adapted from Kainth, J.S., and Verma, H.V. 2011. "Consumer perceived value: Construct apprehension and its evolution."*Journal of Advanced Social Research* 1, no.1, pp. 20–57.

Table 3.4 Similarity in value dimensions

Type	Similar dimensions (source/year)	Type	Similar dimensions (source/year)
Benefits	Quality (Petrick 2002)	Sacrifices	Monetary price (Petrick 2002)
	Quality/performance (Sweeney and Soutar 2001)		Price (Naumann 1995)
	Functional value (Sheth, Newman, and Gross 1991)		Functional price (Hall et al. 2000)
	Functional (William and Soutar 2000)		Perceived risk (Hall et al. 2000)
	Product/service (Naumann 1995)		Behavioral (non-monetary) price (Petrick 2002)
	(Naumann 1995)		
	Functional (Minna Pura 2003)		
	Functional (Heinoen 2004)		
	Functional quality (Hall et al. 2000)		
	Utilitarian (Babin, Darden, and Griffin1994)		
	Extrinsic (Holbrook 1996)		
	Emotional response (Petrick 2002)		
	Emotional (Sweeney and Soutar 2001)		
	Emotional (Sheth, Newman, and Gross 1991)		
	Emotional (William and Soutar 2000)		
	Emotional (Minna Pura 2003)		
	Emotional/social (Hall et al. 2000)		
	Hedonic (Babin, Darden, and Griffin 1994)		

(Continued)

Table 3.4 Similarity in value dimensions (Continued)

Type	Similar dimensions (source/year)	Type	Similar dimensions (source/year)
Benefits	Intrinsic (Holbrook 1996)		
	Price/value for money (Sweeney and Soutar 2001)		
	Reputation (Petrick 2002)		
	Image (Naumann 1995)		
	Social (Sweeney and Soutar 2001)		
	Social (William and Soutar 2000)		
	Social (Sheth, Newman, and Gross 1991)		
	Social (Minna Pura 2003)		
	Social/Emotional (Hall et al. 2000)		
	Epistemic (William and Soutar 2000) Epistemic (Sheth, Newman, and Gross 1991)		
	Conditional (Minna Pura 2003) Conditional (Sheth, Newman, and Gross 1991)		
	Communication (Naumann 1995)		
	People (Naumann 1995)		
	Place (Naumann 1995) Spatial (Heinoen 2004)		
	Temporal (Heinoen 2004)		

Source: Adapted from Kainth, J.S., and Verma, H.V. 2011. "Consumer Perceived Value: Construct Apprehension and its Evolution." *Journal of Advanced Social Research* 1, no.1, pp. 20–57.

theory various researchers have developed a questionnaire as a standardized procedure in a given research premise. The procedure for generating the question has begun with preliminary investigation of the construct in a small group of consumer sampled from the target population. Using a qualitative tool such as focus group interviews were conducted with sample respondents in two to five rounds along a preset list of questions.

The responses of first round were content analyzed and mapped to items in the standard questionnaire to be administered to a larger representative pool of sample respondents. Responses that raise items most engendered into agreement discussion and enthusiasm were used. The choice of sampling technique and tool to collect data is within the discretion of researchers based on the research premise, design, and methodology. Full range of data collection methods are available to researcher, mail survey, telephone interview, and personal interview which could be self administered or interviewer administered. Different statistical analysis procedure such as factor analysis, discriminant analysis, and so on have been used for analysis of data.

Except for a few studies that have tried to develop a scale/index for measuring perceived value, studies have largely operationalized the construct through a generated instrument. The PERVAL and SERVPERVAL scale are the two scales worth mentioning at this stage.

PERVAL

The PERVAL scale was developed by Sweeney and Soutar 2001. It originally consisted of 19 items with a shorter scale developed in 2014 by Walsh et al. the preceding section has elaborated the different directions taken by academic research on value. Keeping the conceptual background on Sheth et al. work on consumption values the scale has considered both the utilitarian and experiential aspect of value. Unlike other previous studies this study is focused on measuring customer perceptions of value of consumer durable goods prior and soon after the purchase as an aid to understand consumer's decision processes and choice behavior. Sheth et al. had argued that consumption value dimensions are independent. They relate additively and their contribution to customer choice is incremental. However, Sweeney and Soutar considered the interrelationship of hedonic and utilitarian characteristics and proposed that value dimensions may not be independent and incremental. Thus their study allowed the value dimensions to be interrelated. The author has also distinctly differentiated between the two constructs of Perceived Value and Satisfaction. Perceived value occurs at various stages of the purchase process whereas Satisfaction has been agreed upon as essentially a post purchase construct. Satisfaction has been found to be dependent on experience of having used the product or service. Value perceptions may occur at any of the stages; purchase, pre- purchase or post-purchase and be varied across stages. Satisfaction has been conceptualized as a summary variable unidimensional in nature moving on the hedonic continuum of unfavorable to favorable. Perceived value has been conceptualized as a multidimensional construct for scale development. The authors separated quality from the price attributes related to the product's functional value of reliability and durability. These were taken together with price by Sheth et al. in their study under functional value. The purpose of the authors was to develop a useful, parsimonious, and practical scale that could be applied to a variety of purchase situations. The rigorous process followed by the authors was based on Churchill (1979) approach for developing measures of multiple item marketing constructs. Two purification stages, one with student sample and another with a more diverse set of customers were done after the development of an initial set of items. The resultant scale was a psychometrically and theoretically validated stable scale. Interested readers may access the details of scale development in the article, the study was done in several rounds in the context of a consumer durable product at brand level in Australia for a population of working and retired people aged 25–59 years.

The following items were considered in the scale.

Factor 1: Quality

1. Has consistent quality
2. Is well made
3. Has an acceptable standard of quality
4. Has poor workmanship
5. Would not last a long time
6. Would perform consistently

Factor 2: Emotional

7. Is one that I would enjoy
8. Would make me want to use it
9. Is one that I would feel relaxed about using
10. Would make me feel good
11. Would give me pleasure

12. Is reasonably priced
13. Offers value for money
14. Is a good product for the price
15. Would be economical

Factor 4: Social

16. Would help me to feel acceptable
17. Would improve the way I am perceived
18. Would make a good impression on other people
19. Would give its owner social approval

The scale clearly highlights that consumers assess products both in functional terms of expected performance, versatility, and value for money and in terms of enjoyment or pleasure received from the product along with the social consequences. The authors recommend that retail marketers must be able to develop more sophisticated positioning strategies by understanding the importance of the different dimensions of value. The limitations of the scale are its generalizability to different contexts beyond the particular product/brand contexts in consumer durable goods and regions. The scale has not considered epistemic and conditional value as in model developed by Sheth et al.

With so much literature review it is worthwhile to note there has been no study that would conceptualize customer perceived value in the BOP context, neither has been one in the Indian context. To summarize:

1.   The goal of marketing is to deliver value
2.   Marketing needs to be all inclusive in nature
3.   Qualitative Research findings
4.   Gap in the literature on family decision making
5.   Gap in the literature on customer perceived value

All the five are important from the BOP perspective and there is an academic and practitioner gap.

For the Indian urban BOP in all roles family is an important dimension as emerging from qualitative study. The Marketing 4 A framework is an inclusive framework but has to adapt the family dimension to serve the BOP.

Market researchers observed that the measurement instruments such as PERVAL which were available for the measurement of the tangible products do not capture value of a service (Jayanti and Ghosh 1996; Petrick 1999). There has been a lot of debate on tangible vs. intangible products such as services. The service dominant logic ends the debate and the book has taken that rationale. The context howsoever is important and with the logic the SERV PERVAL scale that has been developed for services by Petrick et al. 2002 is described here. Unlike the PERVAL scale which considers pre-purchase, purchase and post-purchase stages the SERV PERVAL instrument considers post-purchase stage and repurchase intention. The basic conceptual model of the instrument takes on one of the roles of perceived value in the assessment of the service. It suggests that perceived service quality led to purchase of the service and its subsequent experience (Figure 3.8). The perceived value is formed out of the experience starting point of which is service quality. Service quality is a multi-attribute construct defined by five dimensions:

- Reliability
- Tangibles
- Responsiveness
- Assurance
- Empathy

The customer has expectations on each of the quality attribute and is satisfied if these are met for a specific product in a given context. The perceived value would influence the purchase intention to reinvest in the service experience. It also impacts how positively or negatively the individuals talk to each other about their consumption/service experience. This process would have an effect on the individual's future service quality assessment. The SERV PERVAL scale would only measure perceived value after a purchase and its impact on consumer decision making for future intentions.

```
┌─────────────────────────────┐
│   Perceptions of service    │◄──┐
│          quality            │   │
└─────────────────────────────┘   │
             │                     │
             ▼                     │
┌─────────────────────────────┐   │
│    Purchase of a service    │   │
└─────────────────────────────┘   │
             │                     │
             ▼                     │
┌─────────────────────────────┐   │
│     Service experience      │   │
└─────────────────────────────┘   │
             │                     │
             ▼                     │
┌─────────────────────────────┐   │
│   Perceived value of a      │   │
│   service                   │   │
│   • Behavioural price       │   │
│   • Monetary price          │   │
│   • Emotional response      │   │
│   • Quality                 │   │
│   • Reputation              │   │
└─────────────────────────────┘   │
             │                     │
             ▼                     │
┌─────────────────────────────┐   │
│   Repurchase intention and  │   │
│       word of mouth         │───┘
└─────────────────────────────┘
```

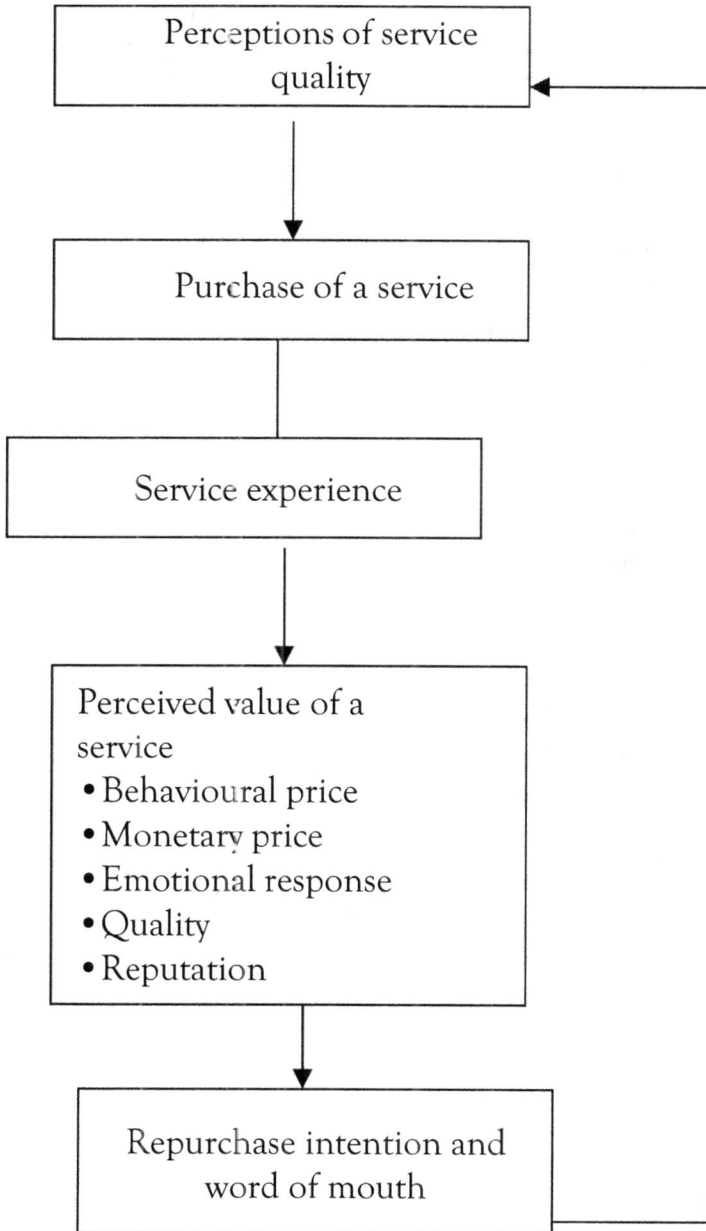

Figure 3.8 Framework for SERV PERVAL scale
Source: Petrick, J.F. 2002. "Development of a Multi Dimensional Scale for Measuring the Perceived Value of a Service." *Journal of Leisure Research* 34, no. 2, pp. 119–34.

The instrument developed through a rigorous procedure identified five values in the pure services context measured through 25 items, mentioned as below:

Factor 1: Quality

1. Is outstanding quality
2. Is very reliable
3. Is very dependable
4. Is very consistent

Factor 2: Emotional Response

5. Makes me feel good
6. Gives me pleasure
7. Gives a sense of Joy
8. Makes me feel delighted
9. Gives me happiness

Factor 3: Monetary Price

10. Is a good buy
11. Is worth the money
12. Is fairly priced
13. Is reasonably priced
14. Is economical
15. Appears to be a good bargain

Factor 4: Monetary Price

16. Is easy to buy
17. Required little energy to purchase
18. Is easy to shop for
19. Required little effort to buy
20. Is easily bought

Factor 5: Reputation

21. Has good reputation
22. Is well respected
23. Is well thought of
24. Has status
25. Is reputable

The authors have mentioned the following limitations in their research;

- Context is very specific, only one sector (tourism and service), needs to move beyond that
- The authors have suggested to explore the interrelationship between factors to refine the perceived value construct.

There is a need to conceptualize customer perceived value in the BOP context across different economies and develop a measurement instrument.

With all the discussion to establish the importance of perceived value, its relevance to firms and context, a marketing framework identified that should facilitate exchange of value between the firm and the customer to meet the objectives at both end, a few cases on each of the four value dimensions are presented where firm have been successful, even if they have not consciously adopted the 4 A framework in the Indian BOP context. After this is done Chapter 4 would then detail how the firms need to then start building on customer engagement for the long term in the urban BOP context.

For achieving marketing outcomes at the BOP, marketers would have to craft effective marketing strategies that give perceived value to the customers. As already detailed in Chapters 2 and 3 customers play multiple roles for a product purchase decision. It has been evident through primary research that perceived value across stages of purchase decision (pre, during, and post) consider the family as an anchor and not individuals in the emerging market such as India especially in the BOP context that was studied. The four key values which the marketers deliver as per the framework outlined earlier are: Awareness, Acceptability, Affordability, and Accessibility. In their respective roles of seeker, payer, user, and influencer customer looks through the family lens to capture each of the four values. This is an important part because if this is missed then the entire effort of the company may be futile. This section would elaborate successful marketing cases at the BOP emphasizing how company delivered perceived value to the customer through the 4As including the family dimension.

Awareness-
Kankhazura Tesan

Before customer can purchase a product they must know about the product and be aware of the brand and its positioning. But this is not sufficient for a customer to make a purchase. Effective advertising should kick-start a process where customer's latent need is hit and he can be stepwise directed toward a purchase. It is important here to understand the role of media vehicles in this process. The advertising and other marketing communication tools utilize a whole set of media vehicles such as television, radio, Internet, bill boards, hoardings, and so on. The media vehicles may differ for different income segments based on income and regions. Such segments may show different consumer behaviors as well. Marketing companies targeting the BOP segment would have to identify the media behaviors and devise their marketing communication accordingly to reach these customers.

Hindustan Unilever Ltd is one of the India's largest fast moving consumer goods company operating in more than 20 categories and over eight decades of experience in India. The company in order to reach low income customers in central India devised a unique strategy. The states of Bihar and Uttar Pradesh are media dark states because of low reach of television and radio coupled with huge power cuts but these states are also the most populated ones with a large BOP segment. Advertising has been important for FMCG companies but it was a big challenge to reach out to this big population segment. However, mobile penetration was almost 40 percent in these areas growing at the rate of 20 percent in 2012. The effective reach of this medium was more than the reach of television and radio the more popular vehicles for HUL's other segments. HUL also had a consumer insight that these low income customers used their mobile calls not for making calls but also for entertainment (radio and stored music content).

Many customers in India had a habit of placing a call on their mobiles and hanging up before the call could be picked up. Their missed call would be returned by the receiver on seeing the number and if he felt the call was worth it. Friends and families would place missed call to save money. HUL decided to convert this frugal behavior with the entertainment consumption part to reach to this customer segment. It developed a missed call campaign strategy for its low cost detergent powder brand targeted at this segment. The brand message for Wheel, the detergent powder brand was around giving more washes at lower cost which met the need of this segment. Every wheel detergent powder packet carried the print, "Make a missed call and stay smiling." On making a missed call at this number mobile users would receive a call back with Bollywood popular Hindi music along with a recorded dialogue from a new movie release of Salman Khan. Salman Khan had a huge mass appeal in this segment which followed his brand endorsement of Wheel. There were movie posters created by HUL for the missed call campaign on the mobile platform by HUL. This was done with the purpose of leveraging the consumer excitement around the new movie release. The content was unique, customized for regional preferences in the dialects of different locations. It was done based on the identification of caller's telecom circle. Apart from the packets the toll free number was promoted through various channels in print and radio. Outbound calls and text messages were also sent to the target customer group. Most of the target customers used prepaid mobile phones and were used to the habit of missed call. The campaign received huge success with five million missed calls from 0.77 million unique users in three months after the launch. There was huge brand engagement achieved with six missed calls per number and 80 percent of customers listening to full ad content. Per contact cost was US $0.04, lower than any other mass media and engagement of 150 seconds per caller, much higher than any other media mode. Based on the success of this activation led to launch of HUL Kankhazura Tesan (KKT) in 2014. KKT was India's first on demand entertainment mobile radio station. The customer gave a missed call to the 1,800 uniques 11 digit number. They received a call within 15 minutes that would feed the caller with free radio offering music, news, jokes and latest Bollywood news. It was interspersed with radio advertisement's of HUL's mass consumer brands. Thus KKT was an immediate success with reaching eight million people in Bihar in first six months. Through this medium HUL could directly engage with the customers for its brand circumventing the challenge of low penetration of other media platforms, power supply and other cultural issues.

Acceptability
Chik Shampoo

Market success can be assured when organizations are sound with the essentials. One such essential element as per the 4 A framework is acceptability. For an offering to be really accepted by the customer the offering has to offer much more than the core solution. Needless to mention that the offering would have to meet and exceed both the customer needs and expectations. As already mentioned acceptability would take two dimensions: functional and psychological. The functional one concentrates on the products whereas the psychological one concentrates on the customer experience. Companies will have to work on both of these. One such interesting example is of Chik Shampoo. Chik Shampoo has been considered as the pioneer of the sachet revolution in India. Started by C.K. Ranganathan, Chairman and Managing Director of CavinKare an INR 1,450 crore company. "Ranganathan's father Chinni Krishnan was a school teacher and used to say: whatever I make must be affordable for the poor man." Whatever the rich man enjoys the poor man should also be able to afford. Basically a school teacher who had shifted to family pharma business had failed in the initial efforts of packaging talcum powder and Epsom salt in sachets. The seed of sachet revolution were still sown. Many low income customers who could not afford a shampoo bottle but wanted to clean their hair by the convenient shampoo had an immediate requirement. Washing hair with shampoo was a new trend catching on in India. People in cities had started using shampoos but the low income customers still had to make the switch. Thus to help them try the shampoo, sachet was introduced. Ranganathan purchased a shampoo packaging machine with an initial investment of Rs. 15,000 and launched Chik shampoo after his father Chinni Krishnan. There were a lot of hurdles initially but in the first month itself he was able to make profits and sold 20,000 sachets. The shampoo sachets were not direct competition to the FMCG giants such as Unilever which were the leaders in the category with the products available mostly through stores. Chik was made available through roadside stalls and grocery outlets not targeted in the urban centers but countryside towns and villages. Ranganathan had got both the packaging and pricing right which made the product acceptable to the customers. He started with Tamil Nadu but slowly was accepted pan India. The product was taken well in terms of size that made it suitable and trial able for the entire family. For a family of five washing hair once a week the cost came less than Rs. 20 per month as the product then was used only by females. Like the high income groups shampoo offered them an easy and convenient way of washing hair while including them in the category. This was a departure for the BOP segment from the traditional methods of hair wash. Rangathan engaged them through a lot of BTL marketing communications event. This made them aware about the product. CavinKare care then launched talcum powder, hair oil, and so on, also in sachets infusing beauty consciousness in the low income customers along with a solution. The shampoo sachet costs were further lowered to 50 paise as cost was one of the company's strengths. Competition entered almost ten years later by when the company had gained a strong ground and got time for establishing systems and practices. The growth of CavinKare has been gradual and focused. By selling shampoo at 50 paise per sachet the company had actually hit gold at the bottom of the pyramid. The company was very good in managing costs through IT solutions and never a compromise on quality was done.

Affordability
Coca Cola India

In 2002–2003 Coca Cola India slashed the prices for its carbonated soft drink brands such as Coke, Thumsup, Limca, Sprite, and Fanta. The vision was to lead the beverage revolution in India and maximize the company's presence in the non-alcoholic carbonated beverages category. The 200 ml and 300 ml packs comprised 70 percent of the consumption basket of Mumbai, the city of launch. The prices were slashed to INR 5 and INR 8 for 200 ml and 300 ml bottles respectively. The company had the insight that per capita consumption of soft drinks in India was very low even in the developing economies. There was a huge untapped market opportunity but affordability was an important concern. Affordability would mean both financial and psychological affordability. Psychologically the target customer in the low income consumer segment was willing to purchase but financial affordability was a problem. The company encouraged financial affordability through the rate cut. The then Regional Operations Director for Coca Cola said,

> this is in keeping with our policy to enhance the affordability factor and increase availability of our products. The lower prices provided an opportunity to a larger section of consumers to experience our world class products on a regular basis.

The market had untapped potential and growth rate was higher than other segments. The company had already achieved some success with the launch of 200 ml bottles. Coca Cola at that time had 58 percent market share in India. In 2004 because of huge distribution and logistics costs the company had to increase the price of 200 ml and 300 ml bottles to INR 7 and 8, respectively. The expense did not affect the family and was easily accommodated in the budget.

Accessibility-
Avon Cosmetics, Brazil

Avon entered South Africa in 1990s at that time the country was rife with aspirant entrepreneurs. The reason for this was that huge formal job creation did not meet the rising levels of labor participation. Informal employment accounted for the bulk of the job creation (Dorris and Thurlow 2009). The informality was highly gendered with women being more self-employed. They were largely engaged with informal business that focused on hawking agricultural produce or traditional handicrafts. This is a very common scenario in India as well. Also, it was largely black women in South Africa that was engaged in informal economic businesses. There were several financial, educational, infrastructural, sociocultural and gender based conditions that kept these women confined to marginally profitable forms of organized trade. Avon saw a unique market opportunity that would take its products to the BOP market spread over a wide and tough terrain while making the women engage as entrepreneurs in its direct sales program. The cost of entry was low and so was the risk of participation in the Avon programme. Today, Avon is one of the largest companies in Brazil and leverages 800,000 "Avon ladies" as distributors to reach the remotest areas and jungles of Amazonia. The Avon system targets women as beneficiaries both in the roles of customers and as sales persons/agents. There was a firm realization in the company that investing in women was the most effective way to improve household, social, and financial health of nations. Most of the FMCG goods were purchased and used by women and they played an important role in these decisions. Access of such products and upscale brands was limited in these regions. At the time of joining Avon gave credit to the participating women. The company would fill orders as they come and did not charge any interest on the credit. Most women began by completing small orders such as a tube of moisturizer, a can of body spray, and so on, they then convert the profit from the small scale into subsequently larger orders. The representative received a commission of 20 percent on the retail price on a sliding scale based on the volume of goods sold. The success of the model was on the insight that women need these products to look and feel beautiful and the kind of access that the women distributors and customers received. Women had the need for these products even in the remotes areas which people could not travel or reach to. The participating women were also responsible for recruitment and administration of other women which would in return make them earn a commission as well. Thus we see how accessibility to the entire household and community was sought by the company through the enterprising women in Brazil.

Conclusion

It is important to run a concept through an implementation framework. The framework should be appropriate and robust to fit in a context. The 4As framework fits well and is robust enough because of its measurement framework. This has been elaborated through the applications of the framework in the chapter.

CHAPTER 4

Institutionalizing Customer Engagement at the Urban Bottom of the Pyramid in India: Research Insights

Introduction

This chapter builds on the relationship between customer engagement (CE) and customer perceived value (CPV); the two customer side marketing constructs that lead to satisfaction. The earlier three chapters detailed on the concept of value, CPV at bottom of the pyramid, and marketing framework for delivering value. This particular chapter takes a long term view to value and talks of how firms can institutionalize CPV and engagement at the bottom of the pyramid in India.

Customer Engagement

CE can be seen as an important success factor for business organizations in the fast paced, dynamic, and contemporary business environment (Verhoef et al. 2010, Kumar and Pansari 2016). It is mostly in the last seven to eight years that the construct has received scholarly attention as organizations realized that engaging with customers is a viable way for enhancing brand and firm performance (Gartner 2014). Gallup research found that on a per-trip basis, fully engaged customers in the consumer electronics industry spent $373, compared to $289 by the actively disengaged customers (Sorenson and Adkins 2014). Thus with the scope for creating successful financial performance outcomes firms tend to be more inclined to engage with their customers. CE denotes "a psychological state that occurs by virtue of interactive customer experiences with a focal object (e.g., a brand) in service relationships" (Brodie et al. 2011). CE has been held as a strategic imperative facilitating sales growth, superior competitive advantage, and profitability (Bijmolt et al. 2010). Engaged customers not only show display greater brand loyalty and satisfaction (Jaakkola and Alexander 2014) but are also more likely to contribute to new product development (Haumann et al. 2015), service innovation (Kumar et al. 2010), and viral marketing activity by providing referrals for specific offerings to others (Chandler and Lusch 2015). The concept has been included in the Marketing Science Institute's 2014–2016 and 2016–2018 Research Priorities (MSI 2014 2016) which emphasizes the relevance and importance of the topic. Additionally, leading journals have brought out Special Issues addressing CE, including the *Journal of the Academy of Marketing Science* (2017), *Journal of Service Research* (2010, 2011), and the *Journal of Consumer Psychology* (2009). Broadly research till date has presented CE conceptualizations (Hollebeek et al. 2014), fundamental propositions of CE (Brodie et al. 2011), measurement instruments applicable to particular CE contexts (Sprott et al. 2009), initial insight into CE antecedents, dynamics and consequences (Van Doorn et al. 2010), and the effect of CE on firm performance (Kumar and Pansari 2016). While CE has been studied in the developed countries and organized business contexts, there has been only one study in the Emerging Markets context that includes India but none on India exclusively or on BOP. The Base of the Pyramid (BOP) segment in India is estimated to be a USD 1.2 trillion market, out of a global USD 5 trillion BOP market excluding China (study by IFC and World Resources Institute). In purchasing power parity terms, the Indian BOP market contributes to about 85 percent of the total national household market (Sinha and Sheth 2017). While the opportunity is huge, the challenges of an informal economy have not let businesses utilize this potential to the full. Managing and overcoming the typical characteristics of emerging markets, such as market heterogeneity, sociopolitical governance, unbranded competition, chronic resource shortages, and inadequate infrastructure, require deep market insights. These insights can be developed through research specific to the Indian BOP market and cannot rely on findings obtained from research on the developed economies or in a different BOP context (Barki and Parente 2006). Poor people are inclined to be more loyal because they cannot afford to make mistakes with their small disposable incomes. As the per capita income and aspirations of this segment increases, it is important that the customers remain loyal to the company and thus Brands and Engagement would play a vital role in the journey. There definitely needs to be a desire in the marketer's mindset to accept this segment as a legitimate target along with a profit orientation. The poor can serve both as creative entrepreneurs/producers and consumers through which companies can cocreate solutions and reduce costs (Karnani 2007). As already mentioned CE and experience has been one of the market research priorities of MSI and though literature has covered several engagement concepts in the discipline, it is important to understand and apply them in the BOP context.

This initiative is the first one that would extend the CE construct to the Indian Urban BOP, with an implementation framework. The first major contribution of the study would be to include CPV in the CE framework developed by Kumar et al. (2017). CPV has been identified as a central mediating construct between firm value and customer value (Kumar and Reinartz 2016) but CPV is different in different income segments including BOP as seen in the earlier chapters. This has been established through a quantitative study based on a staple product brand in the wheat flour category which is consumed by both the segments. The study then builds the drivers for CPV at the BOP which would lead to satisfaction and emotional attachment thus contributing through the direct and indirect contributions of CE provided the firm would have an interaction and omnichannel orientation considered along with the moderators. This would be the second major contribution in terms of extending the CE framework. Only once these are done the study considers the third contribution through proposing a model built on institutional theory that could help firms implement engagement in a long term with this segment. In the last part through different case illustrations from different sectors how the framework can be implemented is described.

Evolution of Customer Engagement

The SD logic is inherently relationship oriented. Based on SD Logic Customer engagement goes beyond cognition and unlike involvement requires the satisfying of experiential value, as well as instrumental value that should result in willingness of both the firm and the customer to continue interactions with each other. Despite Engagement been studied in social sciences, its admission into the Marketing Literature has been a recent one and is still undergoing conceptual refining. As cited by Brodie et al. 2011 in the extensive literature review of CE, the most wide-ranging definitions acknowledging the existence of cognitive, emotional, and behavioral dimensions comprising the CE concept have been provided by authors including Patterson, Yu, and de Ruyter (2006), Vivek, Beatty, and Morgan (2012), Hollebeek (2011), and Mollen and Wilson (2010). The authors have drawn from literatures from related fields (e.g., social psychology) to develop their definitions. Developing on organizational behavior research, Patterson, Yu, and de Ruyter (2006) propose four specific CE components, including (a) absorption: the level of customer concentration on a focal engagement object, such as a brand/organization, thus reflecting the cognitive dimension of engagement; (b) dedication: a customer's sense of belonging to the organization/brand, which corresponds to the emotional dimension of engagement; (c) vigor: a customer's level of energy and mental resilience in interacting with a focal engagement object; and (d) interaction: the two-way communications between a focal engagement subject and object. The latter two dimensions (i.e., "vigor" and "interaction") reflect the behavioral dimension of engagement. In contrast, Vivek, Beatty, and Morgan (2012), view CE from a primarily behavioral perspective by focusing on specific actions and interactions. Specifically, the cognitive and emotional dimensions of engagement identified in the literature review are implied only by the term "connection" in the authors' proposed definition. Mollen and Wilson (2010) view online "brand engagement" to comprise the dimensions of "sustained cognitive processing," "instrumental value" (i.e., utility and relevance), and "experiential value" (i.e., emotional congruence with the narrative schema encountered in computer-mediated entities). The authors also distinguish the concept from "involvement." Specifically,

CE is suggested to extend beyond involvement in that it encompasses a proactive, interactive customer relationship with a specific engagement object (e.g., a brand). Bowden (2009) describes CE as "a psychological process" driving customer loyalty, while Van Doorn et al. (2010) and Pham and Avnet (2009) focus on specific CE behaviors by defining the concept primarily with reference to the specific types and patterns of focal engagement activities. Thus literature review indicated a prominence of the multidimensional (i.e., cognitive, emotional, and behavioral) perspective of engagement. However, despite the prominence of the multidimensional perspective, over 40 percent of the definitions reviewed in the academic and business practice literature expressed engagement as a unidimensional concept and as such, focused on either the emotional, or cognitive, or behavioral aspect of engagement. The behavioral dimension in particular, appears dominant within the unidimensional perspective. However, although the unidimensional approaches possess the merit of simplicity, they fall short in reflecting the rich conceptual scope of engagement. All the different ways of customer value contribution to the firm have been accommodated in the conceptualization of CE (Kumar et al. 2010; Van Doorn et al. 2010). Within the CE concept, studies have investigated topics such as a customer's direct and indirect contributions (Pansari and Kumar 2017), interactive and cocreative experiences (Brodie et al. 2011), value cocreation (Jaakkola and Alexander 2014), and consciousness (Grewal et al. 2017), among others. In defining/explaining CE, studies have adopted various perspectives. For instance, Kumar et al. (2010) adopt a value-based perspective and define CE as active interactions of a customer with a firm, with prospects, and with other customers, whether they are transactional or non-transactional in nature. Van Doorn et al. (2010) adopt a behavioral perspective and define CE as a customer's behavioral manifestation toward a brand or firm, beyond purchase, resulting from motivational drivers. Brodie et al. (2011) adopt a multidimensional perspective and define CE as a psychological state that occurs by virtue of interactive, cocreative customer experiences with a focal agent/object (e.g., a brand) in focal service relationships. Finally, Hollebeek et al. (2016) extends Brodie et al. (2011) definition by adopting a S-D logic perspective to define CE as "a customer's motivationally driven, volitional investment of focal operant resources (including cognitive, emotional, behavioral, and social knowledge and skills), and operand resources (e.g., equipment) into brand interactions in service systems." This definition of CE is adopted for the study. As detailed by Kumar et al. (2017), the CE concept has been effectively adapted and developed to conceptualize and investigate several topics. Table 4.1 displays representative CE studies in the marketing literature. CE has been conceptualized in scientific literature as a context specific phenomenon (Hollebeek 2011 and Brodie 2013). It was found that the expression of particular CE dimensions depends on the subjects of engagement and the context, defined by specific circumstance. So various research on this topic in various service settings and different countries are necessary in order to know the CE phenomenon in more detail.

While there has been only one study in the developing countries context there has been no CE study in the BOP context which may be different not only in terms of business and academic context but also in terms of research design and methodology context. For the purposes of this study the urban Indian BOP comprises of participants primarily engaged in the unorganized sectors and belonged to the 20 percent of the Indian BOP population, but immediately next to the consuming class in metros. The average household size was 5–6 members and average household income per month was INR 25,000–30,000 in 2018 that is, around 30$ a day. The household owned basic facilities such as a rented accommodation either with a television set/refrigerator, a mobile phone per person.

Research Gap, Propositions, and Organization of the Study

Kumar et al. (2017) have developed a framework for CE based on Hollebeek 2016 definition of CE aligned to the Service Dominant logic (that inherently believes that service is the fundamental basis of any exchange and matches with the researcher's orientation). The framework can be applied in both developed and developing countries context. The framework elaborates how interaction orientation and omnichannel model can be used to create positive Service Experience that can lead to CE based on Satisfaction and development of Emotional Bonds, breaking

Table 4.1 Representative CE studies in marketing

Author	Context/orientation (developed markets/ emerging markets/ base of the pyramid)	Nature of the study (conceptual/ empirical)	Research focus	Outcome
Patterson et al. (2006)	Developed markets	Conceptual	Drawing on literature from management, marketing, applied psychology and practitioner's viewpoint a working definition of CE is formed	CE is conceived as a higher order construct consisting of 4 components; vigor, dedication, absorption and interaction
Vivek, Beatty, and Morgan (2012)	Developed markets	Conceptual	Explores the nature and scope of CE	Define CE as the intensity of an individual's participation in and connection with an organization's offerings and/or organizational activities, which either the customer or the organization initiate
Mollen and Wilson (2010)	Developed markets	Conceptual	Reconciles the practitioners' view of engagement as central to online best practice and the scholarly view that tends to use other constructs to assess consumer experience. Building on research in e-learning as well as online marketing	Construe engagement as a cognitive and affective commitment to an active relationship with the brand as personified by the website, and propose S dimensions of this construct

(*Continued*)

Table 4.1 Representative CE studies in marketing (Continued)

Bowden (2009)	Developed markets	Conceptual	Propose a CE framework based on the extent to which customers are either new or repeat purchase customers of a specific service brand	Account for the depth of customers' emotional responses to consumption situations that lead to loyalty and repeat purchase
Kumar et al. (2010)	Developed markets	Conceptual	Propose that the customer's engagement value (CEV) is comprised of their purchase behavior, incentivized referral of new customers, behavior to influence other customers' purchase behavior, and value added to the firm by feedback	Suggest appropriate metrics for measuring the various components of CEV, and propose relationships between the different components of CEV
Van Doorn et al. (2010)	Developed markets	Conceptual	Develop a conceptual model of the antecedents and consequences of CEBs that relate to customer, firm, and society	Propose a CEB management process where firms identify, evaluate and react to key CEBs
Brodie et al. (2011)	Developed markets	Conceptual	Explore the theoretical foundations of CE based on the relationship marketing theory and the S-D logic	Identify five fundamental propositions of CE, and distinguish the concept from other relational concepts
Vivek et al. (2012)	Developed markets	Conceptual	Propose that CE is composed of cognitive, emotional, behavioral, and social elements, and identify the antecedents and consequences of CE	Highlight the importance of understanding individuals' connections with each other relative to the brand, regardless of whether they are purchasing or even considering purchasing the brand

Table 4.1 *Representative CE studies in marketing (Continued)*

Hollebeek (2011a)	Developed markets	Conceptual	Propose a conceptual model to explain the relationships between customer brand engagement (CBE) and other marketing constructs	Identify potentially differential consumer behavior outcomes across the proposed segments of customers
Hollebeek (2011b)	Developed markets	Empirical	Conceptualize CBE using literature and research techniques	Define CBE as the level of a customer's cognitive, emotional and behavioral investment in specific brand interactions
Hollebeek (2013)	Developed markets	Empirical	Explore how CE may contribute to generating customer value (CV) and ensuing loyalty for utilitarian and hedonic brands	Found (a) a curvilinear relationship between CE/CV for utilitarian and hedonic brands; and (b) up to a level, increasing CE generates greater CV for hedonic, than for utilitarian brands
Jaakkola and Alexander (2014)	Developed markets	Empirical	Conceptualize CEB in value cocreation within a multi stakeholder service system	Proposes that CEB affects value co-creation through customers' resource contributions toward the firm/stakeholders that augment the offering
Hollebeek et al. (2016)	Developed markets	Conceptual	Develop an integrative, S-D logic informed framework of CE comprising three CE foundational processes	Develop a set of revised S-D logic–informed FPs of CE, and apply the revised FPs to CRM to generate managerial insights

(Continued)

Table 4.1 *Representative CE studies in marketing* **(Continued)**

Harmeling et al. (2017)	Developed markets	Empirical	Define customer engagement marketing, and propose a framework to show how engagement marketing drives long-term CE	Identify universal characteristics of engagement marketing, differentiate it from other marketing strategies, and offer a typology of two types of engagement marketing (task-based and experiential) that can drive long-term CE
Grewal et al. (2017)	Developed Markets	Conceptual	Propose that consciousness as a foundational philosophy can be used by firms to create a more engaging and meaningful customer experience	Propose that companies can enhance their customer engagement by building on foundations of consciousness, and presents an approach for firms to develop business strategies.
Pansari and Kumar (2017)	Developed markets	Conceptual	Propose a CE framework, and identify its antecedents (satisfaction and emotion) and consequences (tangible and intangible outcomes)	When a relationship is satisfying and has emotional connectedness, the partners become engaged in their concern for each other, as evidenced through direct and the indirect contributions of CE

Table 4.1 Representative CE studies in marketing (Continued)

Kumar et al. (2017)	Developed and emerging	Conceptual	Develop a framework to ensure CE in services by adopting a customer-centric approach	Explores how interaction orientation and omnichannel model can lead to the creation of positive service experience, and identifies the moderators of service experience. Also proposes that the perceived variation in service experience moderates the effect of service experience on satisfaction and emotional attachment
Gupta et al. (2018)	Developed and emerging	Conceptual	Develop a framework for engaging customers globally	Discusses how cultural and economic factors, play a key role in creating global CE for MNCs
Present study	Emerging and BoP	Conceptual	Develops a framework to implement customer engagement at the bottom of the pyramid that is, low income consumers by extending the institutional theory and taking the customer perspective by putting the construct of customer perceived value	Incorporate the customer perspective in CE framework by including the customer perceived value construct as an antecedent to CE in the framework developed by Kumar et al. Based on this the framing of the offering to the BoP can be done, where 3 models have been illustrated

*Adapted from Kumar et al. 2017

into direct and indirect contributions from Engagement; the latter part developed by Pansari and Kumar 2017. The study also identifies the factors that moderate Service Experience categorized as; Offering Related, Value Related, Enablers Related, and Market Related. While the researchers have mentioned that Market Type plays a moderating role and adopting the framework in the emerging markets context may pose certain challenges while also having considered the Perceived Service Offering Complexity yet it stops there. The research has been done on a global scale using Grounded Theory Methodology. However, one major limitation of the study is that though it is customer oriented in nature it has only approached CE through the firm's point of view. CE is a two way process and necessarily needs to be seen from the perspective of the customer for two reasons. First following the cocreation logic customer has to be a part for creating value for himself and thus engaging with the firm. His perspective has only to come from him and not through the organization's perception of his understanding. A good point to start on this is CPV. Second, while studies have built link between CPV and Satisfaction there are many studies that highlight gaps created in satisfaction because of the gap in company's perception of CPV and their drivers. A case in the point is proven by the Knowledge Gap in the Gaps model of Service Quality (Parasuraman, Zeithaml, and Berry 1985) and accordingly gaps have been created in designing and delivery to customer

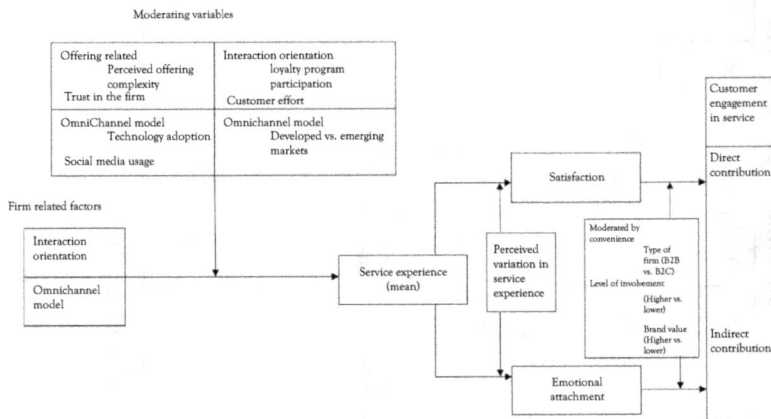

Figure 4.1 Customer engagement framework, Kumar et al. 2017

expectations. Kumar et al. 2017 (Figure 4.1) study though scientifically robust and rigorous faces this limitation as nowhere does it highlight the care taken to remove this bias that may have set in. In fact unless until, the customer's concept of value from the concerned product/brand is considered and their drivers understood by the organization there would continue to be gap in customer satisfaction and repeat purchase intentions. It becomes imperative thus to involve the customer side also in the CE framework across segments, including BOP. This study starts from this perspective.

Customer Engagement Is Linked to Customer Perceived Value

The construct of CPV is not new to the Marketing literature. In fact it has been studied in both goods and services setting till the advent of SD Logic in 2004. One of the most important tasks in marketing is to create and communicate value to customers to drive their satisfaction, loyalty, and profitability. Value is a dual concept with the customer perspective on one side and firm on the other. While the CE framework developed by Kumar et al. does take the firm side of it which is customer oriented in an emerging market context, CE essentially is a two way phenomenon and the customer side also needs to be build in it. The construct of CPV is the construct from the customer side that is linked to long term CE. The subject of CPV, has been studied with different perspectives in Marketing where there has been a strong emphasis on the unidimensional conceptualization of value around utility maximization mainly because of its simpler implementation and assessment (Sanchez-Fernandez and Iniesta-Bonillo 2007), but the multidimensional proposition has gained wider acceptance. The multidimensional conceptualization is a richer one that postulates that consumption experiences involve more than one type of value such as affective or emotional dimensions along with cognitive and economic aspects (Sheth et al. 1991; Babin, Darden, and Griffin 1994 and Holbrook 1994); CPV can thus be summarized as the customer's net valuation of the perceived benefits accrued from an offering that is based on the costs that they are willing to give up for the needs that are seeking to satisfy (Kumar and Reinartz 2016). This definition would consider the multidimensional nature of CPV. There has been a conscious debate over the third stage of conceptualization of CPV over the nature of indicators formative vs. reflective. CPV is considered as a consequence and antecedent to satisfaction in literature Mollen and Wilson (2010), Hollebeek (2013), Brodie et al. (2013). This is because of the difference in the conceptualization where some researchers have considered it at the fulfillment stage and some right from the start stage but there definitely is a linkage between CPV and CE. For the purpose of this study we would consider the process of CPV from the prepurchase stage itself that begins on the get component when the customer starts looking for a specific set of consumption values and builds expectations around them with fulfillment happening at the Satisfaction stage. CPV is the basis for all marketing decisions. Analysis performed by Gummerus (2013) and Khalifa (2004) revealed that CPV is a complex, context specific phenomenon, which still requires attention from the researchers. CPV in marketing literature is being analyzed twofold: as a ratio between customer's value received and cost experienced when purchasing and/or using service/product (e.g., Petrick 2002; Wang et al. 2004; Smith and Colgate 2007) or as a multidimensional construct incorporating various CPV dimensions (e.g., Sweeney and Soutar 2001; Smith and Colgate 2007; Park and Ha 2015). The number of dimensions and their expression depend on the research context and on the purpose of the researcher. However, the majority of research on CPV assumes that value perceptions affect all buyers equally. Few studies have examined consumer heterogeneity in relation to value (Ruiz, Castro, and Armario 2007; Floh, Zauner, Koller, and Rusch 2014), and its explanatory power regarding behavioral intentions. This is surprising, as an aggregate analysis of CPV, disregarding heterogeneous consumer preferences (sub-populations), might result in misleading parameter estimates and inferior managing decisions (Desarbo et al. 2001). One of the key characteristics of Emerging Markets such as India is market heterogeneity apart from sociopolitical governance, unbranded competition, chronic resource shortages, and inadequate infrastructure. Since the Urban BOP has never been studied formally in India the study starts by attempting to understand what constitutes Perceived Value for them.

Customer Perceived Value Is Different Across Segments

The subject of Marketing is about satisfying customer needs profitably. To undertake this task it must be able to understand customer needs and expectations. It is equally important to have an understanding of the customer resources that can be sacrificed to meet those needs. Thus the difference between the "get vs. give" component is what should constitute value for him that may lead to satisfaction. This concept is covered under the "Perceived Value" construct in the Marketing Science. The construct is the same in the BOP context as well as detailed in the previous chapters but the difference would be in the value elements and the context. The CPV framework talks of different value elements as benefits that a customer expects with reference to his purchase context, dependent on the product category minus the cost elements. Scholars have highlighted that CPV is contextual and thus should be different even for the same product categories in different contexts such as lifestyle, lifecycle stage, geography, income, and so on. It typically includes values such as functional, social, emotional, epistemic, and conditional (Sheth et al. 1991). To start with it becomes imperative for the firms targeting the urban metro centers in India for the BOP customer to identify what would constitute Perceived Value for their specific product(s) on these elements and importance given to each one of them. Firms that may not do this may suffer because of marketing myopia and would also not be able to make use of the opportunities available in the urban Indian BOP segment. An exploratory comparative study of 30 Urban Indian BOP (per annum salary around INR 30,00,000) and middle and upper middle income groups (INR 40,00,00 and above) was done in the city of Gurugram India in May–June 2018, to identify the difference in the perceived value. It was decided to do the study on a product category that was relevant and common to both of the segments. Wheat Flour commonly referred as "Atta" forms the staple food in North India which is consumed by both segments. Branded Atta is new category in India, whereas earlier it was sold as loose commodity item which was purchased by user as per his requirement rather than standard packages. Food is a big business in the organized set up which has huge growth potential. Many FMCG majors have entered the segment with branded variants. ITC, the popular FMCG company in India and a leader in the Branded Atta category with major sales from North India partnered for the study. Since branded atta is still in the growth stage, the company was keenly interested in understanding the urban BOP segment as this was the immediately next segment after the SEC A segment which was consuming their products. ITC wanted to identify the opportunity and understand what would constitute Perceived Value for this segment and how does it contrast with its present target segment. Due to exposure to similar lifestyle and conditions for living, the Urban BOP segment which had aspirations to become like the upward classes and work for them have similar needs of convenience and ease of access which makes branded products such as ITC Aashirwaad valuable for them. It also catered to their esteem related needs. ITC wanted to explore this particular segment to continue being the market leader in this segment and catch them young to build brand loyalty. The company shared the attributes related to lifestyle that it used for marketing to current target segment which cut across the five consumption values. Although the customers in the urban BOP segment were catered to mainly by the unorganized or local businesses, but there was availability of infrastructure which could be shared between both the segments by organized businesses. This was different than the rural markets where infrastructure was not developed or present at all in certain locations. 45 percent of the Indian households, 121 million households or around 600 million population is Urban BOP referred to as the next billion by BCG report 2015. The similarities in exposure result in them being aware and having a similar set of expectations around the benefits of atta as a category with their middle and upper middle income group counterparts. Thus the reasons to buy were similar. The difference was in the associated customer costs with each reason which was a constraint for them mainly because of lower incomes as compared to the other group. While they had high expectations on all items related to functional benefits, emotional benefits, service and personnel benefits, image related psychological benefits, there was a difference in their payment capabilities, which could be because of willingness or ability to pay as their income was different. Companies would thus have to rework their cost and resource structures as existing structures would not be able to provide value either to the customer or to the firm itself. Thus

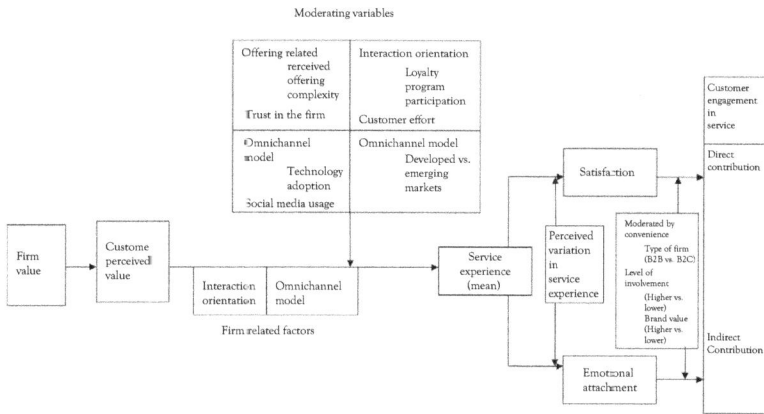

Figure 4.2 Modified customer engagement framework, Kumar et al. 2017

to generate value for both the customer and the company, companies will have to start by identifying the CPV and its elements in the specific context and then find innovative ways to incorporate them in business models that are implementable. In a long term CE context companies not only need to understand CPV but also need to work out the drivers for CPV so that the customers remain satisfied and engaged in the long term. This is exactly the stage of urban BOP in India. Thus to build an implementable CE framework CPV has to be included as an antecedent in the CE model developed by Kumar et al. along with the interaction and omnichannel orientation in the presence of moderators.

The Drivers for CPV Are Important

To understand the drivers for CPV at the Urban BOP, a grounded theory study was done amongst a select sample of 15 participants in the urban Gurugram, a part of NCR of Delhi. Semi-structured in-depth interviews were conducted with them in their native language that is, Hindi. The details of the study are mentioned in Chapter 2. The two drivers for the CPV identified for the bottom of the pyramid Indian urban customer were "concern for family" and "concern for price." For any product including wheat flour, whether ITC Aashirwaad or any other they derived satisfaction when their needs related to these two were fulfilled. To develop CE, these two concerns have to roped in the market offering of the firm. The family dimension in the bottom of the pyramid urban customer tilted toward economic well-being rather than subjective well-being as observed in other upper income segments. After the drivers have been identified implementation frameworks needs to be built for CE which is what has been developed in the next section on institutionalizing CE at the BOP.

Institutionalizing Customer Engagement at the Bottom of the Pyramid

Prabhu et al. (2017) elaborate how Marketing has been defined as a social and managerial process by which individuals and groups obtain what they need and want through creating and exchanging products and values with others. Kotler et al. (2008) and essentially marketing is the study of how firms create and maintain exchanges with customers (Bagozzi 1974, 1975; Hunt 1983; Houston and Gassenheim 1987; Vargo and Lusch 2004), but, marketing to the poor in emerging markets poses significant challenges that do not exist in developed economies (Mahajan and Banga 2006; Wu 2013). They have further illustrated how the institutions required for the creation and maintenance of exchanges are often non-existent or fragmented in emerging markets (Khanna and Palepu 2000). Specifically, these markets frequently lack the institutions that help with assessing customer preferences (e.g., market research firms that specialize in poor segments) and responding to customer preferences (e.g., the absence of a distribution and sales infrastructure that reaches the poor) (Prahalad 2010). The attempt to create and maintain exchanges with the poor in emerging economies therefore requires a different approach to marketing than in developed economies (Pauwels et al. 2013). Prabhu et al. 2017 have developed a model to examine the creation and maintenance of exchanges with the poor in emerging economies that has the possibility of being extended to CE in the Urban India BOP context to work out an implementation framework. The authors have first tried to identify why marketing to the poor in emerging markets entails a unique set of challenges relative to marketing in developed economies. To respond to these unique challenges (e.g., the lack of institutions that facilitate formal exchange) would require the creation of new business models through institutional entrepreneurship, namely working with existing institutions to create an environment that enables the business model. The authors have adopted an institutional lens to build a framework that would facilitate marketing exchange to the poor in developing economies and the same holds true for CE. There are large numbers of low income consumers who have an increasing ability and desire to consume and are thus attractive customer segments to serve and engage in long term. But, marketing to these segments presents firms from both developed and emerging economies with some severe difficulties because of which their existing models face market failure. Market failure has been described as a situation in which there is inefficient allocation of goods and services in a market (Ledyard 2008), which could be because of demand side failures: lack of awareness, lack of accessibility, and lack of affordability (Prahalad 2010; Anderson and Markides 2007; Anderson et al. 2010; Kashyap and Raut 2006; Mahajan 2008; Mahajan and Banga 2006). The authors have also identified three supply side reasons for market failure: lack of awareness of a given market opportunity, lack of the means to reach poor consumers, and the lack of an economical means of initiating and fulfilling exchange with such consumers (Prahalad 2010; Anderson and Markides 2007; Anderson et al. 2010; Kashyap and Raut 2006; Mahajan 2008; Mahajan and Banga 2006). Thus, there exist other forms of exchange and engagement which would leave buyers better off than the existing forms available. It is here that firms like ITC will have to become Institutional Entrepreneurs to affect institutional change so that they can enter into long term CE. Based on institutional theory the following steps need to be undertaken to build an implementation framework at BOP (Figure 4.3).

1. **Framing**: Frames are shared interpretive schemes or systems of meaning that help actors make sense of the world and provide templates for organizing (McAdam et al. 1996), which may be taken for granted by the constituent actors in that context. On the other hand, institutional entrepreneurs can challenge dominant frames through the development of strategically constructed alternatives. This essentially has to be done on the CPV with a long term CE orientation in mind. The modified CE conceptual framework (Figure 4.2) would

be converted to the implementation stage (Figure 4.3). As reiterated by Prabhu et al. institutional entrepreneurs would need to engage in three main framing tasks when seeking to alter a particular system of meaning (Benford and Snow 2000). The first task is diagnostic framing, in which a particular problem is articulated along with the attempt to identify the causes of the same. The second task is prognostic framing, in which a potential solution to the articulated problem is identified along with the steps. The third core framing task is motivational framing. This stage provides the rationale or justification for a particular course of action through which institutional entrepreneurs can galvanize support and convince others to commit time and effort toward a particular goal. Thus the companies can use a framework that can guide them right from design till implemen-

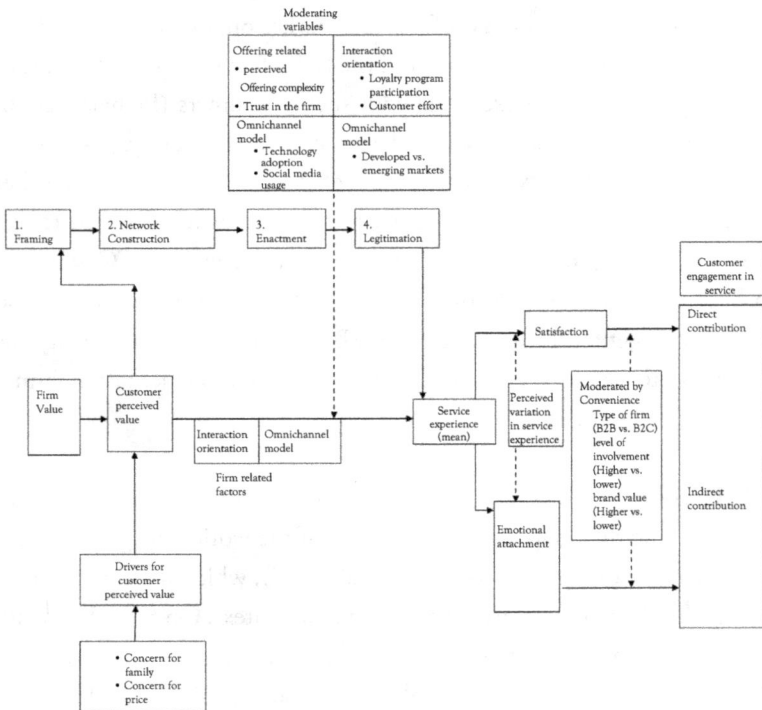

Figure 4.3 An Integrated Institutional Model for Implementing CE at BoP in Urban India

tation of CE in an urban India BOP context. This insight and the framing task is the most critical for building long term CE. It has been elaborated through three cases in the subsequent section.

2. **Network construction**: The next step in the implementation process is network construction which is a political process characterized by competition and cooperation between the relevant actors in a given institutional setting (Hargrave and Van de Ven 2006).

3. **Enactment of institutional arrangements**: the third step is enactment of institutional arrangements which entails working with powerful state and other regulatory actors in order to create or enact the formal and informal institutions necessary for a given business model innovation to become viable, and

4. **Legitimation**: Through collective action processes, legitimation would involve proving that the business model works by getting consumers and other stakeholders committed to the new form of exchange and ensuring that the resources needed to sustain the model continue to flow toward it.

Cases

FMCG: Hindustan Unilever Ltd.

If correct framing is done then companies can identify needs around existing practices to come up with new models. This is what Hindustan Unilever did in Project Shakti across rural India. The customers in rural India were denied day-to-day FMCG products because of the supplier bottleneck. The rural infrastructure was very poor in the year 2009 in India. FMCG companies that require intensive distribution faced major challenges here because it could not channelize the urban machinery of sales force to rural India. Thus "Accessibility" was an important dimension for CPV. In such a context through prognostic framing, Hindustan Unilever decided that instead of replicating the urban distribution infrastructure in rural India, it should develop a new model using resources from amongst rural India. This is a very important point, instead of fitting one model in another frame, develop model that arouses out of that frame. It launched the innovative project Shakti—using rural women.

The key idea was that women is a strong influential force in rural house-holds and tapping the women would work in favor of the company as she would be able to convince her household and community. Second and even more important element that Hindustan Unilever considered in this project was the problem of unemployment and livelihood. Project Shakti opened a new avenue of employment of not the men but the women folk who was not even considered for employment in the traditional structures and systems of this society. There was also an underlying logic that rural folks also needed these products with a slight difference in their needs but were denied because of a lack of suitable infrastructure. Thus the company clubbed two unrelated needs and worked out a solution that offered greater CPV with long term engagement and resolved both the supply and demand side issues. The HUL team selected few women leaders who were called Shakti Ammas. These Shakti Ammas were actually women entrepreneurs attached to a Self Help Group. The Shakti Ammas were trained for familiarization with the products and basic tenets of distribution management and basics of management that would enable them to run their business effectively. Project Shakti now has nearly 80,000 micro-entrepreneurs across 18 states.

Voluntary Sector: The Art of Living

NGOs or not for profit societies are organizations with a cause but not for commercial reasons (profits) alone. The "Art of Living" organization promoted by Sri Sri Ravishankar, a spiritual and humanitarian leader, is such an organization. The mission of the society is to create and empower peace and humanitarian values in the society through the Indian ancient technique of yoga and seva (service). Though the basic nature of the organization may seem to be spiritual in nature yet the organization undertakes regular activities covered by business and government otherwise in the sectors of rural development/women empowerment, health/education, and so on broadly catering to the development of the underdeveloped regions across the world. Their target regions include the bottom of the pyramid customer; both urban and rural. They take up causes that relate to human development in a holistic approach. People from well-to-do segments are given the responsibility of executing development projects related to the BOP customer. Thus the organization also fills an important psychological gap in the well to do people. Through a community based approach they integrate well to do segments that can devote time, money and effort in their projects in rural areas (education/health etc.) on the demand side. Thus through diagnostic, prognostic, and motivational framing a community based model works that offers greater perceived value to the BOP people while also meeting the needs of the suppliers.

Informal Sector: Urban Domestic Household Help in Urban India

The Indian culture being collectivist in nature was used to living in joint families With the change in employment opportunities, being now available only in the metros for both skilled and unskilled labor the urban lifestyles have changed. In the earlier traditional model, families for generations used to continue at their native places in the same jobs whether agriculture or service. The proportion of agriculture/farming related jobs was higher and spread throughout the country. With the opening of Indian economy the Indian urban centers grew disproportionately and both skilled and unskilled labor was drawn to these leaving other places. In such a scenario with both spouses working there was a new need of Household care for dependents. These families could afford to pay but did not have time. Thus they could either outsource by sending the dependent to a day care or old age home or in source by hiring domestic help on a full time or part time basis. Many middlemen were involved but basically the workers were immigrants from undeveloped areas that lacked employment opportunities. They were not professionally educated, some had a level of school education mostly basic and a significant proportion was illiterate. Whether hired through middlemen or directly they worked in the category of household care doing regular cleaning, cooking, and nursing of dependents (young or old). Though unorganized in nature, apart from the regular salary their working terms included stay and meals. This model is now a common feature in all urban metros with MNC employees. The traditional model only paid for the labor against a specific task but here they were paid for their time and availability at the home in case a need arose. Thus the engagement happened through innovations in the framing part of CPV that clubbed two unrelated needs.

It is not only unorganized sectors but on relating this to e-commerce space we would find support that even those organizations are reaping success because of Framing the unrelated needs in their business model through technology. All e-commerce business value propositions are framed on the need of removing the physical travel to the store/home delivery through anytime anywhere convenient ordering. Thus even organized businesses would innovate but identifying the innovations around a specific need is the first important step. The context of BOP customer is different than upper and middle income customer in India and therefore the CPV is also different. Only after this step is undertaken under Diagnostic framing can firms be able to deliver and engage with the customers in the long term. The focus of organized business both because of opportunity and implementation has been based on some specific segments that could afford to pay for the costs involved or benefits received. This can continue but for the urban BOP they will have to start by identifying what constitutes CPV as there is no existing practitioner or academic literature specifically for them. This has been done in an isolated manner but has to be taken forward in a more structured manner from now by both business and academia.

Discussion and Conclusion

CE has been recognized as one of the most important contemporary marketing topics. Researchers globally are trying to study the topic and its related dimensions in detail with reference to business practices in different contexts. One such context is low income consumers in developing and underdeveloped countries commonly referred to as the Base/bottom of the pyramid customer. The challenges in this segment are unique and huge for established corporate which makes it difficult to replicate their business models. Marketing as a science has its origin in the developed markets but the BOP market offers immense scope against their saturating existing markets. To cater to this market, marketing scholars and practitioners have started acknowledging and understanding this market. The process has just started. While the importance and uniqueness of this market is appreciated it is also required to be studied in its own right. The urban Indian BOP market is also one such context which has been studied in this book through a fresh perspective and is the need of the hour. The characteristics and novelty of the market demand a novel research approach as opposed to structured approaches. While statistical methods would be used more as the research matures in these market but the present phase calls for a qualitative focus using certain unconventional methods and a combination of them such as, interpretative phenomenology, grounded theory, case method, and so on which have been used in social sciences research. The present study follows a mixed method approach using a combination of quantitative descriptive study coupled with grounded theory and case study method. The first important contribution of the study is the inclusion of the CPV, CPV in the CE framework developed by Kumar et al. for institutionalizing CE, that is, working out an implementation framework in Urban India BOP the first important step for organized business is to identify what constitutes CPV for their particular offering. CPV is essentially net benefits minus costs. Due to a difference in lifestyle and living conditions because of income difference the low income consumers differ in their consumption and spending habits. This does not mean they are unaware or less aware or are less in their aspirations but this mainly because of the difference in their resource availability and disposition. This leads to a difference in the CPV of the customers in this segment vs. other segments. Major FMCG companies in India are interested in understanding the BOP urban India segment as this forms the immediate next segment with opportunity for their products and is currently being served largely by unorganized business. The importance can be witnessed by the fact that the company ITC, whose product Aashirwaad is a market leader in branded wheat flour category in North India, where this forms the staple diet got involved right from the problem formulation stage and worked continuously through research design and findings stage. The findings established that CPV is different for the brand across BOP and other higher income groups. The difference primarily is on the costs side than the benefits side which was similar in terms of customer expectations from the brand. Thus for a long term CE the brand will have to start investing in framing their offerings to appeal to this customer segment. The main drivers for CPV were two in this segment that led to customer satisfaction as revealed in the next phase of the study through grounded theory. The two main drivers were "concern for family" and "concern for money." They were different in terms of their orientations as compared to other segments which focused on the "subjective well being" of the family whereas BOP focused on "economic well being." Once this part is incorporated in the existing CE framework by Kumar et al., companies can start building their offerings for CE through the extension of institutional theory integrated with this. Prabhu et al. have developed a marketing implementation model based on Institutional theory for creating marketing exchanges with poor customers in developing economies/emerging markets. The new CE framework developed is integrated with this framework to develop a long term implementation CE framework for Urban India BOP customer. Once CPV is determined organizations will have to start playing the role of institutional entrepreneurs. They would now have to do the task of framing their market offering for CE. Through case illustrations three successful case studies from different sectors highlight how organizations challenged the fitment of existing frames through diagnostic framing, generated new frames by essentially clubbing two unrelated needs that would bring the organizations more close to the customers and use his resources differently to give him returns more than the immediate product. This step is called prognostic framing and is inherently aligned with the SD logic which treats customer resources differently. The next step is motivational Framing where the customer is convinced and motivated to not only purchase the firm's products but is engaged to give his resources and cocreate value to satisfy his direct/indirect needs which is way beyond his expectation. The next steps of network construction and enactment of institutional arrangements are more process related. Thus a long term implementation framework of CE is established in the urban India BOP context.

Future Research

The present study may be seen as the start of a journey and not as an end in itself. It is an attempt to study the vast population at the BOP in a specific country context. The implementation framework developed may be tested empirically. Also there is a need to test it in other BOP segments in other emerging markets context.

References

CHAPTER 1

Achrol, R.S., and P. Kotler. 1999. "Marketing in the Network Economy [special issue]." *Journal of Marketing* 63, pp. 146–163.

Austin, J.E., H.B. Leonard, E. Reficco, and J. Wei-Skillern. 2008. "Social entrepreneurship: it is for Corporations, Too." In *Social Entrepreneurship: New Models of Sustainable Social Change*, ed. A. Nicholls, 169–204. Oxford: Oxford University Press.

Bamford, M. 2011. "Are MINTS the Next Big Investment Opportunity." from http://abrmr.com/myfile/conference_proceedings/Con_Pro_32717/conference_67356.pdf (accessed April 28, 2019)

BCG. 2002. "Mercados pouco explorados: descobrindo a classe C." Boston Consulting Group: São Paulo.

Conner, K.R., and C.K. Prahalad. 1996. "A Resource-Based Theory of the Firm: Knowledge vs Opportunism." *Organization Science* 7, pp. 477–501.

Constantin, J.A., and R.F. Lusch. 1994. *Understanding Resource Management.* Oxford, OH: The Planning Forum.

Day, G.S. 1999. *The Market Driven Organization: Understanding,Attracting, and Keeping Valuable Customers.* New York, NY: The Free Press.

Elg, U., P. Ghauri, and V. Tarnovskaya. 2008. "The Role of Networks and Matching in Market Entry to Emerging Retail Markets." *International Marketing Review* 25, no. 6, pp. 674–699.

Erich, W.Z. 1951. *World Resources and Industries*, New York, NY: Harper and Brothers, Revised edition

Floh, A., A. Zauner, M. Koller, and T. Rusch. 2014. "Customer Segmentation Using Unobserved Heterogeneity in the Perceived-Value–Loyalty–Intentions Link." *Journal of Business Research* 67, pp. 974–982.

Garcia-Herrero, A., Navia, D. and M. Nigrinis. 2010. *BBVA EAGLEs.* (BBVA Research: Cross-Country Emerging Markets Analysis Economic Watch, 15 November). Madrid, Spain.

Ghauri, P.N. 2004. "Designing and Conducting Case Studies in International Business Research." In *Handbook of Qualitative Research Methods for International Business,* eds. R. Marschan-Piekkari and C. Welch, 107–124. Edward Elgar, Cheltenham.

Ghauri, P.N., V. Tarnovskaya, and U. Elg. 2008. "Market Driving Multinationals and their Global Sourcing Network." *International Marketing Review* 25, no. 5, pp. 504–519.

Guesalaga, R., P. Marshall. 2008. "Purchasing Power at the Bottom of the Pyramid: Differences Across Geographic Regions and Income Tiers." *Journal of Consumer Marketing* 25, pp. 413–418.

Gupta, U. 2011. *MIST: The Next Tier of Large Emerging Economies.* Institutional Investor.

Hakansson, H., and I. Snehota. 1995. *Developing Relationships in Business Networks.* Thomson International, London.

Hamel, G. and C. Prahalad. 1994. "Competing for the Future." *Harvard Business Review.*

Hammond, A.L., and C.K. Prahalad. 2004. "Selling to the Poor." *Foreign Policy* 142, pp. 30–37.

Hammond, A.L., W.J. Kramer, R.S. Katz, J.T. Tran, and C. Walker. 2007. *The Next 4 Billion: Market Size and Business Strategy at the Base of the Pyramid*

Hoskisson, R.E., L. Eden, C.M. Lau, and M. Wright. 2000. "Strategy in Emerging Economies." *Academy of Management Journal* 43, no. 3, pp. 249–267.

http://bostonanalytics.com/images/The-Rising-Bottom-of-the-Pyramid-in-India.pdf

Hunt, S.D. 2000. "Synthesizing Resource-Based, Evolutionary and Neoclassical Thought: Resource-Advantage Theory as a General Theory of Competition." In *Resources, Technology, and Strategy*, eds. N.J. Foss and P. Robertson, 53–79. London: Routledge.

Ireland, J. 2008. "Lessons for Successful BOP Marketing from Caracas' Slums." *Journal of Consumer Marketing* 25, no. 7, pp. 430–438.

Karnani, A. 2007. "The Mirage of Marketing to the Bottom of the Pyramid: How the Private Sector can Help Alleviate Poverty." *California Management Review* 49, no. 4, pp. 90–111.

Karnani, A. 2008. "Employment, Not Microcredit, is the Solution." *Journal of Corporate Citizenship* 32, pp. 23–28.

Karnani, A. 2008. "Help, Don't Romanticize, The Poor." *Business Strategy Review* 19, no. 2, pp. 48–53.

Karnani, A. 2008. "Innovation in Poor Countries." *Issues in Science & Technology* 24, no. 3, pp. 15–17.

Karnani, A. 2008. "Romanticizing the Poor Harms the Poor." *The Whitehead Journal of Diplomacy and International Relations*, 57–70. Summer-Fall.

Karnani, A. 2010. "Failure of the Libertarian Approach to Reducing Poverty." *Asian Business Management* 1, pp. 5–21.

Kolk, A., M. Rivera-Santos, and C. Rufin. 2012. "Reviewing a Decade of Research on the 'Base/Bottom of the Pyramid' (BOP)." *Business & Society* 20, no. 10, pp. 1–40.

Kramer, A.E. 2009. *Emerging Economies Meet in Russia.* The New York Times.

Kumar, V., and A. Pansari. 2016. "Competitive Advantage through Engagement." *Journal of Marketing Research* 53, no. 4, pp. 497–514.

Kuratko, D.F., J.S. Hornsby, and J.S. McMullen. 2011. "Corporate Entrepreneurship with a Purpose: Exploring the Antecedents to Corporate Social Entrepreneurship." *Academy of Management Annual Meeting Proceedings.*

London, T., and S.L. Hart. 2004. "Reinventing Strategies for Emerging Markets: Beyond the Transnational Model." *Journal of International Business Studies* 35, no. 5, pp. 350–370.

London, T., R. Anupind, and S. Sheth. 2010. "Creating Mutual Value: Lessons Learned from Ventures Serving Base of the Pyramid Producers." *Journal of Business Research* 63, no. 6, pp. 582–594.

Madhok, A. 2000. "Transaction (in)Efficiency Value (in)Efficiency, and Interfirm Collaboration." In *Cooperative Strategy: Economic, Business and Organizational Issues*, eds. D. Faulkner, and M.D. Rond, pp. 74–95. Oxford University Press, Oxford.

Maslow, A.H. 1943. "A Theory of Human Motivation." *Psychological Review* 50, no. 4, pp. 370–396.

Maslow, A.H. 1962. *Toward a Psychology of Being.* Princeton: D. Van Nostrand Company.

Maslow, A.H. 1987. *Motivation and Personality, 3rd ed.* Delhi, India: Pearson Education.

McLeod, S.A. 2017. "Maslow's Hierarchy of Needs." Retrieved from www.simplypsychology.org/maslow.html, (accessed April 30, 2019)

Mizik, N., and R. Jacobson. 2003. "Trading Off Between Value Creation and Value Appropriation The Financial Implications of Shifts in Strategic Emphasis." *Journal of Marketing* 67, no. 1, pp. 63–76.

Nthenge, D. 2015. *Bottom of the Pyramid Marketing Strategies, Product Positioning and Consumer Perception.*

Oliveira, Mariana. 2006. *A base da pirâmide torna-se o topo das vendas.* Mundo do Marketing.

O'Neill, J. 2001. *Building Better Global Economic BRICs*, Global Economic Paper #66, Goldman Sachs.

Parvathiyar, A., and J.N. Sheth. 1999. *Handbook of Relationship Marketing.* Sage Publications, Thousand Oaks, CA.

Penrose, E.T. 1996. "Growth of the Firm and Networking." In *International Encyclopaedia of Business and Management*, ed. M. Warner, 1716–1724. Routledge, London.

Perez-Aleman, P., and M. Sandilands. 2008. "Building Value at the Top and the Bottom of the Global Supply Chain: MNC-NGO Partnerships." *California Management Review* 51, no. 1, pp. 24–49.

Polanyi, M. 1958. *Personal Knowledge: Towards a Post-Critical Philosophy.* University of Chicago Press, Chicago.

Porter, M.E. 1985. *Competitive Advantage*, Chapter 1, 11–15. New York, NY: The Free Press.

Prahalad, C.K. 2010. *The Fortune at the Bottom of the Pyramid: Eradicating Poverty Through Profits*. Philadelphia: Wharton School Publishing

Prahalad, C.K. 2012. "Bottom of the Pyramid as a Source of Breakthrough Innovations." *Journal of Product Innovation Management* 29, no. 1, pp. 6–12.

Prahalad, C.K., and A.L. Hammond. 2002. "Serving the world's Poor, Profitably." *Harvard Business Review* 80, no. 9, pp. 48–57.

Prahalad, C.K., and G. Hamel. 1990. "The Core Competence of the Corporation." *Harvard Business Review* 68, no. 3, pp. 79–91.

Prahalad, C.K., and S. Hart. 2002. "The Fortune at the Bottom of the Pyramid." *Strategy+Business* 26, no. 1, pp. 55–67.

Press. https://unitus.vc/resources/defining-base-of-the-economic-pyramid-in-india/ (accessed January 2, 2017)

Ruiz, D.M., C. Castro, and E. Armario. 2007. "Explaining Market Heterogeneity in Terms of Value Perceptions." *The Service Industries Journal* 27, pp. 1087–1110.

Salem Khalifa, A. 2004. "Customer Value: A Review of Recent Literature and an Integrative Configuration." *Management Decision* 42, pp. 645–666.

Sanchez-Fernandez, R., and M.A. Iniesta-Bonillo. 2007. "The Concept of Perceived Value: A Systematic Review of the Research." *Marketing Theory* 7, pp. 427–451.

Sheth, J.N., B.I. Newman, and B.L. Gross. 1991. "Why We Buy What We Buy: A Theory of Consumption Values." *Journal of Business Research* 22, pp. 159–170.

Sinha, M., and J. Sheth. 2017. "Growing the Pie in Emerging Markets: Marketing Strategies for Increasing the Ratio of Non-Users to Users." *Journal of Business Research* 86, pp. 217–224.

Smith, J.B., and M. Colgate. 2007. "Customer Value Creation: A Practical Framework." *Journal of Marketing Theory & Practice* 15, pp. 7–23.

Sorenson, S., and A. Adkins. 2014. "Why Customer Engagement Matters So Much Now." *Gallup*, July 22. Available at http://gallup.com/businessjournal/172637/why-customer-engagement-matters.aspx

Sprott, D., S. Czellar, and E. Spangenberg. 2009. "The Importance of a General Measure of Brand Engagement on Market Behavior: Development and Validation of a Scale." *Journal of Marketing Research* 46, no. 1, pp. 92–104.

Sweeney, J.C., and G.N. Soutar, 2001. " Consumer Perceived Value: The Development of a Multiple Item Scale." *Journal of Retailing* 77, no. 2, pp. 203–220.

Van Doorn, J., K.E. Lemon, V. Mittal, S. Nass, D. Pick, P. Pirner, and P.C. Verhoef. 2010. "Customer Engagement Behavior: Theoretical Foundations and Research Directions." *Journal of Service Research* 13, no. 3, pp. 253–266.

Vargo, S.L., and R.F. Lusch. 2004. "Evolving to a New Dominant Logic for Marketing." *Journal of Marketing* 68, no. 1, pp. 1–17.

Verhoef, P.C., W. Reinartz, and M. Krafft. 2010. "Customer Engagement as a New Perspective in Customer Management." *Journal of Service Research* 13, no. 3, pp. 247–252.

Vivek, S.D., S E. Beatty, and R.M. Morgan. 2012. "Customer Engagement: Exploring Customer Relationships Beyond Purchase." *Journal of Marketing Theory and Practice* 20 no. 2, pp. 122–146.

Wang, Y., H. Po Lo, R. Chi, and Y. Yang. 2004. "An Integrated Framework for Customer Value And Customer-Relationship Management Performance: A Customer-Based Perspective from China." *Managing Service Quality: An International Journal* 14, pp. 169–182.

Wu, J. 2013. "Marketing Capabilities, Institutional Development, and the Performance of Emerging Market Firms: A Multinational Study." *International Journal of Research in Marketing* 30, no. 1, pp. 36–45.

CHAPTER 2

Dey, I. 1999. *Grounding Grounded Theory: Guidelines for Qualitative Inquiry*. San Diego, CA: Academic Press.

Fisk, R.P.P., A. Laurel, E.B. David, G. Thorsten, O. Amy, P. Lia, R. Javier, and S. Roberta 2016. "Billions of Impoverished People Deserve to be Better Served: A Call to Action for the Service Research Community." *Journal of Service Management* 27, no. 1, pp. 43–55.

Gebauer, H., and R. Javier. 2013. "An Agenda for Service Research at the Base of the Pyramid." *Journal of Service Management* 24, no. 5, pp. 482–502

Glaser, B.G. 1978. *Theoretical Sensitivity*. Mill Valley, CA: The Sociology Press.

Glaser, B.G., and A.L. Strauss. 1967. *The Discovery of Grounded Theory: Strategies for Qualitative Research*. Chicago, Aldine Publishing Company.

Hart, S.L., and S. Sharma. 2004. "Engaging Fringe Stakeholders for Competitive Imagination." *Academy of Management Perspectives* 18, no. 1, pp. 7–18.

Heskett, J.L., W.E. Sasser, and L. Schlesinger. 1997. *The Service Profit Chain: How Leading Companies Link Profit and Growth to Loyalty, Satisfaction, and Value*. New York, NY: The Free.

Ireland, J. 2008. "Lessons for Successful BOP Marketing from Caracas' Slums." *Journal of Consumer Marketing* 25, no. 7, pp. 430–438.

Press. https://unitus.vc/resources/defining-base-of-the-economic-pyramid-in-india/ (accessed on 2 January, 2017)

Sheth, J. 2011. "Impact of Emerging Markets on Marketing: Rethinking Existing Perspectives and Practices." *Journal of Marketing* 75, no. 4, pp. 166–182.

Srivastava, R. 2018. "Customer Expectations at the Urban Bottom of Pyramid in India: A Grounded Theory Approach." In *Business Governance and Society - Analyzing Shifts, Conflicts, and Challenges*, ed. Rajagopal and R. Behl. Palgrave Macmillan, New York, NY: In Press.

Zeithaml, Valarie A., Leonard L. Berry, and A. Parasuraman 1968. "Attitudinal Effects of Mere Exposure." *Journal of Personality Social Psychology*, no. 9, pp. l–28.

CHAPTER 3

Aulia, S.A., I. Sukati, and Z. Sulaiman. 2016. "A Review: Customer Perceived Value and its Dimension." *Asian Journal of Social Sciences and Management Studies* 3, no. 2, pp. 150–162.

Belch, G., M.A. Belch, and G. Ceresino. 1985. "Parental and Teenage Influences in Family Decision Making." *Journal of Business Research* 13, pp. 163–176.

Berlyne, D.E. 1960. *Conflict, Arousal, and Curiosity*. New York, NY: McGraw-Hill.

Berlyne, D.E. 1970. "Novelty, Complexity, and Hedonic Value." *Perception Psychophysics* 8, no. 5, pp. 279–286.

Chikweche, T., J. Stanton, and R. Fletcher. 2012. "Family Purchase Decision Making at the Bottom of the Pyramid." *Journal of Consumer Marketing* 29, no. 3, pp. 202–213.

Churchill, G.A., Jr. 1979. "A paradigm for Developing Better Measures of Marketing Constructs." *Journal of Marketing Research*, pp. 64–73.

Commuri, S., and J.W. Gentry. 2000. "Opportunities for Family Research in Marketing." *Academy of Marketing Science Review* 8, pp. 1–34.

Cunningham, I.C., and R.T. Green. 1974. "Purchasing Roles in the U.S. family." *Journal of Marketing* 38, no. 4, pp. 61–64.

Davis, H.L. 1971. "Measurement of Husband-Wife Influence in Consumer Purchase Decisions." *Journal of Marketing Research* 13, pp. 305–312.

Davis, H.L. 1976. "Decision Making Within the Household." *Journal of Consumer Research* 2, pp. 241–260.

Davis, H.L., and B.P. Rigaux. 1974. "Perception of Marital Roles in Decision Processes." *Journal of Consumer Research* 1, no. 1, pp. 51–62.

Filiatrault, P., and J.R. Brent Ritchie. 1980. "Joint Purchasing Decisions: A Comparison of Influence Structure in Family and Couple Decision-Making Units." *Journal of Consumer Research* 7, pp. 131–140.

Hansen, F. 1972. *Consumer Choice Behavior: A Cognitive Theory*. New York, NY: The Free Press.

Hansen, F. 1981. "Hemispheral Lateralization: Implications for Understanding Consumer Behavior." *Journal of Consumer Research* 8, pp. 23–36.

Hirschman, E.C. 1980. "Innovativeness, Novelty Seeking, and Consumer Creativity." *Journal of Consumer Research* 7, pp. 283–295.

Holbrook, M.B. 1983. "Using a Structural Model of Halo Effect to Assess Perceptual Distortion Due to Affective Overtones." *Journal of Consumer Research* 10, pp. 247–252.

Howard, J.A. and J.N. Sheth. 1969. *The Theory of Buyer Behavior.* New York, NY: John Wiley and Sons.

Hyman, H.H. 1942. "The Psychology of Status." *Archives of Psychology* (Columbia University) 269, p. 94.

Jayanti, R.K., and A.K. Ghosh. 1996. "Service Value Determination: An Integrative Perspective." *Journal of Hospitality & Leisure Marketing* 3, no. 4, pp. 5–25.

Joag, S.G., J.W. Gentry, and J.A. Hopper. 1984. "Explaining Differences in Consumption by Working and Nonworking Wives." *Advances in Consumer Research* 11, pp. 582–585.

Kainth, J.S., and Verma, H.V. 2011. "Consumer Perceived Value: Construct Apprehension and its Evolution." *Journal of Advanced Social Research* 1, pp. 20–57.

Katz, E., and P.F. Lazarsfeld. 1955. *Personal Influence: The Part Played by People in the Flow of Mass Communications.* New York, NY: The Free Press.

Kotler, P. 1974. "Atmospherics as a Marketing Tool." *Journal of Retailing* 49, pp. 48–64.

Laura A.W., and A.C. Burns. 2000."Exploring the Dimensionality of Children's Direct Influence Attempts." In *NA - Advances in Consumer Research,* eds. J.H. Stephen and R.J. Meyer, Vol 27, pp. 64–71. Provo, UT: Association for Consumer Research.

Lin, C.H., S.J. Peter, and H.Y. Shih. 2005. "Past Progress and Future Directions in Conceptualizing Customer Perceived Value." *International Journal of Service Industry Management* 16, no. 4, pp. 318–336.

Marshall, A. 1890. *Principles of Economics,* 2nd ed. 1891, 3rd ed. 1895; 5th ed. 1907; 8th ed. 1920; re-edited in 1994. London: Macmill.

Martineau, P. 1958. "The Personality of the Retail Store." *Harvard Bussiness Review* 36, pp. 47–55.

Orstein, R.E. 1972. *The Psychology of Consciousness.* San Francisco: W.H. Freeman.

Park, C.W. 1982. "Joint Decisions in Home Purchasing: A Muddling-Through Process." *Journal of Consumer Research* 9, pp. 151–156.

Park, C.W., and S.M. Young, 1986. "Consumer Response to Television Commercials: The Impact of Involvement and Background Music on Brand Attitude Formation." *Journal of Marketing Research* 23, pp. 11–24.

Petrick, J. F. 2002. "Development of a Multi-Dimensional Scale for Measuring the Perceived Value of a Service." *Journal of Leisure Research* 34, no. 2, pp. 119–134.

Petrick, J.F. 1999. "An Examination of the Relationship Between Golf Travelers' Satisfaction, Perceived Value and Loyalty and their Intentions to Revisit." Dissertation, Clemson, SC: Clemson University.

Qualls, W.J. 1988. "Toward Understanding the Dynamics of House- Hold Decision Conflict Behavior." In *Advances in Consumer Research*, ed. M.J. Houston, Vol. 15, pp. 442–448. Provo, UT: Association for Consumer Research.

Robertson, T.S. 1967. "The Process of Innovation and the Diffusion of Innovation." *The Journal of Marketing* 63, pp. 14–19.

Rogers, E.M. 1962. *Diffusion of Innovations*. New York, NY: Free Press of Glencoe.

Rogers, E.M., and Shoemaker, F.F. 1971. *Communication of Innovations: A Crosscultural Approach*, 2nd ed., New York, NY: The Free Press.

Rosen, D.L., and D.H. Granbois. 1983. "Determinants of Role Structure in Family Financial Management." *Journal of Consumer Research* 10, pp. 253–258.

Sheth, J.N. and R. Sisodia. 2012. *The 4 A's of Marketing: Creating Value for Customer, Company and Society*. Routledge. NY.

Sheth, J.N., B.I. Newman, and B.L. Gross. 1991. *Consumption Values and Market Choice*. Cincinnati, OH: South Western Publishing Company.

Sillars, S., and P. Kalbfleisch. 1988. "Implicit and Explicit Decision-Making Styles in Couples." In *Dyadic Decision Making*, eds. D. Brinberg and J. Jaccard, 179–211. NewYork, NY: Springer Verlag.

Sweeney, J.C., and G.N. Soutar. 2001. "Consumer Perceived Value: The Development of a Multiple Item Scale." *Journal of Retailing* 77, no. 2, pp. 203–220.

Veblen, T. 1899/1912. *The Theory of the Leisure Class: An Economic Study of Institutions*. New York, NY: Macmillan.

Walsh G., E. Shiu, and L.M. Hassan. 2014. "Replicating, Validating, and Reducing the Length of the Consumer Perceived Value Scale." *Journal of Business Research* 67, no. 3, pp. 260–267.

Walsh, G., and V.W. Mitchell. 2010. "Consumers' Intention to Buy Private Label Brands Revisited." *Journal of General Management* 35, no. 3, pp. 3–24.

Warner, W.L., and P.S. Lunt, 1941. The Social Life of a Modern Community. New Haven, CT, US: Yale University Press.

Wilkes, R.E. 1975. "Husband-Wife Influence in Purchase Decisions -- A Confirmation and Extension." *Journal of Marketing Research* 12, pp. 224–227.

Woodruff, R.B. 1997. "Customer Value: The Next Source for Competitive Advantage." *Journal of the Academy of Marketing Science* 25, no. 2, pp. 139–153.

Zajonc, R.B. 1968. "Attitudinal Effects of Mere Exposure." *Journal of Personality Social Psychology*, Monograph Suppf, pp. 1–28.

CHAPTER 4

Anderson, J., and C. Markides. 2007. "Strategic Innovation at the Base of the Pyramid." *MIT Sloan Management Review*, pp. 83–88.

Anderson, J., C. Markides, and K. Martin. 2010. "The Last Frontier: Market

Creation in Conflict Zones, Deep Rural Areas and Urban Slums." *California Management Review* 52, no. 4, pp. 1–23.

Anderson, J., N. Billou. 2007. "Serving the World's Poor: Innovation at the Base of the Economic Pyramid." *Journal of Business Strategy* 28, no. 2, pp. 14–21.

Babin, B.J., W.R. Darden, and M. Griffin. 1994. "Work and/or Fun: Measuring Hedonic and Utilitarian Shopping Value." *Journal of Consumer Research* 20, pp. 644–656.

Bagozzi, R.P. 1974. "Marketing as an Organized Behavioral System of Exchange." *Journal of Marketing* 38, no. 4, pp. 77–81.

Bagozzi, R.P. 1975. "Marketing as Exchange." *Journal of Marketing* 39, no. 4, pp. 32–39.

Barki, E., and J. Parente. 2006. "Consumer Behaviour of the Base of the Pyramid Market in Brazil." *Greener Management International* 56, pp. 11–23.

Benford, R.D., and D.A. Snow. 2000. "Framing Processes and Social Movements: An Overview and Assessment." *Annual Review of Sociology* 26, no. 1, pp. 611–639.

Bijmolt, T.H., P.S. Leeflang, F. Block, M. Eisenbeiss, B.G. Hardie, A. 'lie Lemmens, and P. Saffert. 2010. "Analytics for Customer Engagement." *Journal of Service Research* 13, no. 3, pp. 341–356.

Bowden, J.L. 2009a. "The Process of Customer Engagement: A Conceptual Framework." *Journal of Marketing Theory and Practice* 17, no. 1, pp. 63–74.

Brodie, R.J., A. Ilic, B. Juric, and L. Hollebeek. 2013. "Consumer Engagement in a Virtual Brand Community: An Exploratory Analysis." *Journal of Business Research* 66, pp. 105–114.

Brodie, R.J., L.D. Hollebeek, B. Jurić, and A. Ilić. 2011. "Customer Engagement: Conceptual Domain, Fundamental Propositions, and Implications for Research." *Journal of Service Research* 14, no. 3, pp. 252–271.

Chadler, J.D., and R.F. Lusch. 2015. "Service Systems: A Broadened Framework and Research Agenda on Value Propositions, Engagement, and Service Experience." *Journal of Service Research* 18, no. 1, pp. 6–22.

Desarbo, W.S., K. Jedidi, and I. Sinha. 2001. "Customer Value Analysis in a Heterogeneous Market." *Strategic Management Journal* 22, pp. 845–857.

Floh, A., A. Zauner, M. Koller, and T. Rusch. 2014. "Customer Segmentation Using Unobserved Heterogeneity In the Perceived-Value–Loyalty–Intentions Link." *Journal of Business Research* 67, no. 5, pp. 974–982.

Gartner. 2014. "Gartner Highlights the Four Key Attributes of Customer Engagement." *Gartner*, Inc., Available at http://gartner.com/newsroom/id/2689817, (accessed March 25, 2014).

Grewal, D., A.L. Roggeveen, R. Sisodia, and J. Nordfält. 2017. "Enhancing Customer Engagement through Consciousness." *Journal of Retailing* 93, no. 1, pp. 55–64.

Gummerus, J. 2013. "Value Creation Processes and Value Outcomes in Marketing Theory: Strangers or Siblings?" *Marketing Theory*, pp. 1–29.

Gupta, S., A. Pansari, and V. Kumar. 2018. "Global Customer Engagement: Conceptual Framework and Research Propositions." *Journal of International Marketing*.

Harmeling, C.M., J.W. Moffett, M.J. Arnold, and B.D. Carlson. 2017. "Toward a Theory of Customer Engagement Marketing." *Journal of the Academy of Marketing Science* 45, no. 3, pp. 312–335.

Haumann, T., P. Gunturkun, L.M. Schons, and J. Wieseke. 2015. "Engaging Customers in Coproduction Processes: How Value-Enhancing and Intensity-Reducing Communication Strategies Mitigate the Negative Effects of Coproduction Intensity." *Journal of Marketing* 79, pp. 17–33.

Holbrook, M.B. 1994. "The Nature of Customer Value, An Axilogy of Services in the Consumption Experience." *Thousand Oaks*, CA: Sage.

Hollebeek, L. 2011a. "Demystifying Customer Brand Engagement: Exploring the Loyalty Nexus." *Journal of Marketing Management* 27, nos. (7–8), pp. 785–807.

Hollebeek, L. 2011b. "Exploring Customer Brand Engagement: Definition and Themes." *Journal of Strategic Marketing* 19, no. 7, pp. 555–573.

Hollebeek, L. 2013. "The Customer Engagement/Value Interface: An Exploratory Investigation." *Australasian Marketing Journal* 21, no. 1, pp. 17–24.

Hollebeek, L.D., R.K. Srivastava, and T. Chen. 2016. "S-D Logic–Informed Customer Engagement: Integrative Framework, Revised Fundamental Propositions, and Application to CRM." *Journal of the Academy of Marketing Science*, pp. 1–25.

Houston, F.S. and J.B. Gassenheim. 1987. "Marketing and Exchange." *Journal of Marketing* 51, no. 4, pp. 3–18.

Hunt, S.D. 1983. "General Theories and the Fundamental Explananda of Marketing." *Journal of Marketing* 47, no. 4, pp. 9–17.

Jaakkola, E., and M. Alexander. 2014. "The Role of Customer Engagement Behavior in Value Co-Creation a Service System Perspective." *Journal of Service Research* 17, no. 3, pp. 247–261.

Jensen, J.M. 1990. "Family Purchase Decision Making – A 'Buying Centre' Approach." Doctoral Dissertation, University of Southern Denmark, Odense (in Danish).

Kashyap, P., and S. Raut. 2006. *The Rural Marketing Book (Text/Practice)*. New Delhi: DreamTech Press.

Khanna, T., and K. Palepu. 2000. "Is Group Affiliation Profitable in Emerging Markets? An Analysis of Diversified Indian Business Groups." *The Journal of Finance* 55, pp. 867–891.

Kotler, P., V. Wong, J. Saunders, G. Armstrong, and M.B. Wood. 2008. *Principles of Marketing: Enhanced Media*, European ed. London: Prentice Hall.

Kumar, V., and W. Reinartz. 2016. "Creating Enduring Customer Value." *Journal of Marketing,* 80, no. 6, pp. 36–68.

Kumar, V., L. Aksoy, B. Donkers, R. Venkatesan, T. Wiesel, and S. Tillmans. 2010. "Undervalued or Overvalued Customers: Capturing Total Customer Engagement Value." *Journal of Service Research* 13, no. 3, pp. 297–310.

London, T., and S.L. Hart. 2001. *Next Generation Business Strategies for the Base of the Pyramid: New Approaches for Building Mutual Value.* Upper Saddle River, N.J.: FT Press.

Mahajan, V. 2008. *Africa rising: How 900 million African Consumers Offer More than You Think.* NJ: Wharton School Publishing.

Mahajan, V., and K. Banga. 2006. *The 86 Percent Solution: How to Succeed in the Biggest Market Opportunity of the Next 50 Years.* Upper Saddle River: Wharton School.

McAdam, D., J.D. McCarthy, and M.N. Zald. 1996. "Introduction: Opportunities, Mobilizing Structures, and Framing Processes – Toward a Synthetic, Comparative Perspective on Social Movements." In *Comparative Perspectives on Social Movements,* eds. D. McAdam, J.D. McCarthy and M.N. Zald. Cambridge: Cambridge University Press.

Mollen, A., and H. Wilson. 2010. "Engagement, Telepresence, and Interactivity in Online Consumer Experience: Reconciling Scholastic and Managerial Perspectives." *Journal of Business Research* 63, nos. 9/10, pp. 919–925.

Parasuraman, A., Zeithaml, V. A., and Berry, L.L. 1985. "A Conceptual Model of Service Quality and Its Implications for Future Research." *The Journal of Marketing,* pp. 41–50.

Patterson, P., Y. Ting, and K. de Ruyter. 2006. "Understanding Customer Engagement in Services." *Advancing Theory, Maintaining Relevance, Proceedings of ANZMAC.* Conference, Brisbane, 4-6 December.

Pauwels, K., S. Erguncu, and G. Yildirim. 2013. "Winning Hearts, Minds and Sales: How Marketing Communication Enters the Purchase Process in Emerging and Mature Markets." *International Journal of Research in Marketing* 30, no. 1, pp. 57–68.

Petrick, J.F. 2002. "Development of a Multi-Dimensional Scale for Measuring the Perceived Value of a Service." *Journal of Leisure Research* 34, no. 2, pp. 119-134.

Pham, M.T. and T. Avnet. 2009. "Rethinking Regulatory Engagement Theory." *Journal of Consumer Psychology* 19, no. 2, pp. 115–123.

Prabhu, J., P. Tracey, and M. Hassan. 2017. "Marketing to the Poor: An Institutional Model of Exchange in Emerging Markets." *AMS Review,* 7, nos. 3–4, pp. 101–122.

Reficco, E., and P. Márquez. 2012. "Inclusive Networks for Building BOP Markets." *Business & Society* 51, no. 3, pp. 512–556.

Rondinelli, D.A. and T. London. 2003. "How Corporations and Environmental Groups Cooperate: Assessing Cross-Sector Alliances and Collaborations." *Academy of Management Executive* 17, no. 1, pp. 61–76.

Ruiz, D.M., C. Castro, and E. Armario. 2007. "Explaining Market Heterogeneity in Terms of Value Perceptions." *The Service Industries Journal* 27, pp. 1087–1110.

Santos, F. 2012. "A Positive Theory of Social Entrepreneurship." *Journal of Business Ethics* 111, no. 3, pp. 335–351.

Seelos, C., and J. Mair. 2005. "Social Entrepreneurship: Creating New Business Models to Serve the Poor." *Business Horizons* 48, no. 3, pp. 241–246.

Shaw, E., and R. Tamilia. 2001. *Robert Bartels and the History of Marketing Thought.*

Sheth, J., R.S. Sisodia, and A. Sharma. 2000. "Antecedents and Consequences of the Growth of Customer-Centric Marketing." *Journal of Academy of Marketing Science* 28, no. 1, pp. 55–66.

Sheth, J.N. 2011. "Impact of Emerging Markets on Marketing: Rethinking Existing Perspectives and Practices." *Journal of Marketing* 75, no. 4, pp. 166–182.

Slater, S.F., and J.C. Narver. 1995. "Market Orientation and the Learning Organization." *Journal of Marketing* 59, no. 3, pp. 63–74.

Srivastava, R.K., L. Fahey, and H.K. Christensen. 2001. "The Resource-Based View and Marketing: The Role of Market-Based Assets in Gaining Competitive Advantage." *Journal of Management* 27, no. 6, pp. 777–802.

Tasavori, M., and R.R. Sinkovics. 2010. "Socially Entrepreneurial Behaviour of Multinational Companies: Are MNCs 'Social Entrepreneurs'?" In *Firm-Level Internationalisation, Regionalism and Globalization*, eds. E. Hutson, R.R. Sinkovics and J. Berrill, 397–411. Palgrave Macmillan, Houndmills, Basingstoke.

Tasavori, M., P.N. Ghauri, and R. Zaefarian. 2014. "Entry of Multinational Companies to the Base of the Pyramid: Network Perspective." In eds. C. Jones and Y. Temouri, pp. 39–52. International Business, Institutions and Performance After The Financial Crisis, Palgrave Macmillan.

Teece, D.J., and G. Pisano. 1994. "The Dynamic Capabilities of Firms: An Introduction." *Industrial and Corporate Change* 3, no. 3, pp. 537–556.

Teegen, H. 2006. "Achieving the Millennium Development Goals: Ways for MNCs to Effectively Interface with NGOs." In *Multinational Corporations and Global Poverty Reduction*, eds. S.C. Jain and S. Vachani, pp. 261–285. Edward Elgar, Northampton, MA.

Teegen, H., J.P. Doh, and S. Vachani. 2004. "The Importance of Nongovernmental Organizations (NGOs) in Global Governance and Value Creation: An International Business Research Agenda." *Journal of International Business Studies* 35, no. 6, pp. 463–483.

UNDP. 2008. *Creating Value For All: Strategies For Doing Business with the Poor.* New York, NY: United Nations Development Programme.

UNESCO. 2014. "Education For All Global Monitoring Report, 2013/4 Report Teaching and Learning: Achieving Quality for All." Paris, United Nations Educational, Scientific and Cultural Organization (UNESCO).

Vachani, S., and N.C. Smith. 2008. "Socially Responsible Distribution: Distribution Strategies for Reaching the Bottom of the Pyramid." *California Management Review* 50 no. 2, pp. 52–84.

Vargo, S.L., and R.F. Lusch. 2004. "Evolving to a New Dominant Logic for Marketing." *Journal of Marketing* 68, no. 1, pp. 1–17.

Vaz, D. 2006. *Estratégias de marketing para o consumidor na base da pirâmide*. São Paulo.

Walsh, J.P., J.C. Kress, and K.W. Beyerchen. 2005. "Promises and Perils at the Bottom of the Pyramid." *Administrative Science Quarterly* 50, no. 3, pp. 473–482.

Webster, F.E., Jr. 1992. "The Changing Role of Marketing in the Corporation." *Journal of Marketing* 56, pp. 1–17.

Wilson, D., and A. Stupnytska. 2007. "The N-11: More than an Acronym. (Global Economics Paper No:153)." London: Goldman Sachs Economic Research. Retrieved from https://portal.gs.com

Winter, Sidney G. and R.R. Nelson. 1982. "An Evolutionary Theory of Economic Change University of Illinois at Urbana-Champaign's Academy for Entrepreneurial Leadership Historical Research Reference in Entrepreneurship." Available at SSRN: https://ssrn.com/abstract=1496211

World Resource Institute. 2007. "The Next 4 Billion Market-Market Size and Business Strategy at the Base of the Pyramid." Executive Summary.

World Resources Institute. 2006. "Development through Enterprise Project, & Inter-American Development Bank." *The Market of the Majority: The BOP Opportunity Map of Latin American and the Caribbean*. Washington, D.C: World Resources Institute. Retrieved from http:/wri.org/publication/market-of-the-majorit

Zeithaml, V.A., L.L. Berry, and A. Parasuraman. 1993. "The Nature and Determinants of Customer Expectations of Service." *Journal of the Academy of Marketing Science* 21, pp. 1–12.

Zimmermann, E.W. 1951 *World Resources and Industries,* Revised edition. New York, NY: Harper and Brothers.

About the Author

Dr. Ritu Srivastava is a Faculty and the Area Chairperson, Marketing at Management Development Institute, Gurgaon, popularly referred as MDI Gurgaon. The core of Dr. Srivastava's work centers around the industry with the firm belief that management education at all levels has to be absorbed by the industry. Her research ideas have been appreciated at national and international marketing conferences. Her paper titled, "Employee actions that lead to customer satisfaction: services revisited in India, 2014," was adjudged the best paper at the International Marketing Conference at Fore School of Management, New Delhi, and has been documented in the Academic Reference Series—Reinventing Marketing for Emerging Markets, Bloomsbury India, 2014. Her latest research work revolves around the Indian Consumer in a changed shopping context, which has been adapted as a Textbook on Retailing Management by Pearson, 2017, which is a bestseller. She is an avid case writer publishing with leading publishers such as Richard Ivey School of Business and Emerald Emerging Market Case Studies. She is presently working on the low income customers in India. The low income customers in India represent a big segment for marketers to serve. As a trainer her programs on marketing, services marketing, and marketing communications have been appreciated by the clients and participants. She has been involved with training various organizations such as BEL, DST, DGET, DGR, LIC, NADP, Canon India, and Vodafone. She also has developed a simulation, "Customer Black Box" which is being used by B schools for Marketing Management.

Index

Alphabets '*f*' and '*t*' in *italics* after page numbers indicate figure and table, respectively.

base of pyramid. *See* bottom of pyramid
bottom of pyramid (BOP), 7, 23, 112, 120, 141, 142, 143, 144. *See also* customer engagement
  approach benefits, 28–29
  and customer perceived value, 24–25
  definition, 37
  differing perspectives to, 29–30
  educational issues, 24
  family dimension, 77
  first-generation, 27–28
  importance of in business, 23
  income issues in, 23–24
  infrastructure issues, 24
  market characteristics, 30–31
  marketing strategies for, 31–32
  open codes for consumer behaviour, 63*f*
  premises of Indian consumer, 65–68
  second-generation, 29
  subjective *vs.* economic well being, 71, 144
  and zone of tolerance model, 69*f*
business. *See also* marketing; value chain
  as growth engines, 6–7
  benefit to society, 5
  and concept of value, 7–8, 111
  core processes in, 16
  marketing concepts, 9–14
  objective of, 5, 7
  profit measurement, 8
  and profit, 5
  and shareholder value, 7
  system in India, 6

capital returns
  as a measure of profitability, 8
  net profit, 8
  sources of, 8
capital, 8, 31
capitalism, 6, 7
conditional value, 93, 107
consumption value, 90
  consumption choice behaviour
    conditional value, 93, 107
    emotional value, 92
    epistemic value, 92–93, 107
    functional value, 91
    social value, 91–92
  theory propositions, 90
  value dimensions, 96*t*–102*t*
core competency, 19, 20
customer engagement (CE). *See also* customer perceived value
  as multidimensional engagement, 123, 131
  components in, 122
  and customer loyalty, 123
  and customer perceived value, 131–132
  definition, 120, 123, 124
  framework for bottom of pyramid, 137–139, 138*f*, 143, 144
  framework, 130*f*, 135*f*
  and marketing, 142
  need for, 119
  and service dominant logic, 124
  service experience categories, 130
  usefulness of, 120
customer perceived value (CPV), 1, 22–23, 80, 93*f*, 107, 111, 121, 131, 139, 143
  consumption choice behaviour, 91–93, 105

consumption value, 90
contextual nature of, 133
and customer engagement
   framework, 121
and customer engagement,
   131–132
definition, 22, 89–90
drivers of, 135–136, 143–144
andmarketing mix, 73
measurement of, 104–105
   PERVAL scale, 105–108
   SERV PERVAL scale, 108–111
andorganized sector, 142
segment differences in, 133–134
subjectivevs. economic well being,
   71
and unorganized sector, 141
and urban India bottom of pyramid
   customer, 24–25, 37, 63f,
   65–68, 69f, 71
utilitarian and hedonic model, 94
value dimensions, 96t–102t, 105,
   107, 114, 133
value hierarchy model for,
   93f, 94
zone of tolerance model, 69f

decision-making, family, 80–82, 83,
   105, 107, 132
concept of family, 83–84
consumption choice behaviour,
   91–93
role of children in, 86–87
role of gender in, 85
westernvs. bottom of pyramid
   markets, 83

emerging markets, 31, 120,
   130, 132
characteristics of, 120
as per economic levels perspective,
   27
as per financial growth perspective,
   25–27
and social entrepreneurship, 36
enterprise, 4, 5, 19
as a factor of production, 5, 6
epistemic value, 92–93, 107

4As framework, the, 107, 113
buyer role and value, 76, 83
customer roles, 74, 77f
definition, 77–78
measurement of, 79
payer role and market values,
   75–76
role of family in, 80–82, 105
seeker role, 76
user role and values, 75

grounded theory 60, 130, 144

India, 6, 7, 18, 23, 25, 31, 64, 68, 84,
   85, 86, 107, 120, 132, 141,
   143
integrated marketing, 13
internal vs. external marketing, 13
levels in, 13

market value coverage (MVC), 79
marketing concept
goals, 11
need for, 12
pillars in
   customer needs, 11
   profitability, 11–12
   target market, 11
marketing management, 9
marketing mix, 73
and the 4As framework, 74
marketing, 8–9, 14, 17, 23, 24, 77,
   107, 131, 136, 142. See also
   customer engagement
approaches to, 9, 111
concepts under
   integrated marketing concept, 13
   marketing concept, 10–13
   product concept, 10
   production concept, 9–10
   selling concept, 10, 11, 14
   societal marketing concept,
      13–14
andcore competence, 19–20
definition, 8
inclusive nature of, 17
management, 9
market failure reasons, 137

andmarket failure, 137
operand *vs.* operant resources,
    17–18, 21, 123–124
problems in, 9, 136–137
service marketing thought, 27, 28, 29
service-centered view of, 19, 20
Maslow, Abraham, 1
Maslow's hierarchy of needs, 1, 2*f*
  categories in, 3
  deficiency needs, 2
  growth or being needs, 2
  order in, 4
  priorities in, 3

open codes, 63
operand resource, 17, 124
operant resource, 18, 123

PERVAL scale, 105
  and consumer choice, 205
  factors in, 106–107
  limitation in, 107
  perceived value vs. satisfaction,
    105–106, 108
  vs. SERV PERVAL scale, 108
  and value dimensions, 105
production factors, 5–6, 13

risk capital, 7

SD logic. *See* service-related
    dominant logic
selective codes, 64
SERV PERVAL scale, 108
  concept of, 108
  framework of, 169*f*
  limitations, 111
  vs. PERVAL scale, 108
  and service quality, 108
  values in, 110
service quality, 108
service-centered dominant (SD) logic,
    17, 19, 20, 122, 124
  attributes and premises of, 21, 22
  vs. goods-centered dominant logic,
    21*t*, 73
shareholder, 7
  profitability and profit growth, 8, 11

and risk capital, 7
value, 7,8
social entrepreneurs, 34
  building blocks for, 35–36
  vs. commercial entrepreneur, 35
  and social value creation, 34–35,
    91–92
social value, 91–92
socialism, 6, 7
societal marketing
  objectives, 13
  social and ethical issues in, 13–14
society, 1, 6
  and benefits from business, 5
  needs of, 1
stakeholders, 4
  classification, 4
  needs, 4

theoretical codes, 65

value chain, 15
  core business processes in, 16
  primary activities in, 15–16
  support activities in, 16
value, 1, 6, 9, 14, 15, 17–18, 20, 22,
    23, 34, 35, 73, 74, 91*f*, 105,
    108, 111, 121, 131.
    See also customer perceived
    value; marketing; value
    chain
  availability, 76
  chain, 15
  convenience, 76
  delivery frameworks for, 73
  delivery process, 14–15
  economic, 75–76
  and operand resources, 17, 124
  and operant resources, 18, 123
  performance, 75
  psychological, 75, 114
  social, 75

World Economic Pyramid (WEP), 7,
    28, 31

Zimbabwe, 84
  purchase behaviour, 85

OTHER TITLES IN OUR MARKETING COLLECTION

Naresh Malhotra, Georgia Tech, Editor

- *Service Excellence: Creating Customer Experiences That Build Relationships* by Ruth N. Bolton
- *Relationship Marketing Re-Imagined: Marketing's Inevitable Shift from Exchanges to Value Cocreating Relationships* by Naresh K. Malhotra, Can Uslay, and Ahmet Bayraktar
- *Critical Thinking for Marketers, Volume I: Learn How to Think, Not What to Think* by Terry Grapentine, David Soorholtz, and David Dwight
- *Critical Thinking for Marketers, Volume II: Learn How to Think, Not What to Think* by Terry Grapentine, David Soorholtz, and David Dwight
- *Employee Ambassadorship: Optimizing Customer-Centric Behavior From The Inside-Out and Outside-In* by Michael W. Lowenstein
- *Qualitative Marketing Research* by Rajagopal

Announcing the Business Expert Press Digital Library

Concise e-books business students need for classroom and research

This book can also be purchased in an e-book collection by your library as

- a one-time purchase,
- that is owned forever,
- allows for simultaneous readers,
- has no restrictions on printing, and
- can be downloaded as PDFs from within the library community.

Our digital library collections are a great solution to beat the rising cost of textbooks. E-books can be loaded into their course management systems or onto students' e-book readers.
The **Business Expert Press** digital libraries are very affordable, with no obligation to buy in future years. For more information, please visit **www.businessexpertpress.com/librarians**. To set up a trial in the United States, please email **sales@businessexpertpress.com**.